The Politics
of the
Common Market

W. HARTLEY CLARK, the author of this book, is Associate Professor of Government and International Relations at Carleton College. From 1961 to 1962 he was Fulbright Advanced Research Scholar at the headquarters of the Common Market in Brussels, Belgium.

The Politics
of the
Common Market

W. Hartley Clark

PRENTICE-HALL, INC.
A SPECTRUM BOOK   *Englewood Cliffs, New Jersey*

JN
15
C5

9/6/67 Contr. Spl. 6.95

To Barbara

52647

B. W.

Preface

"We are not in business at all: we are in politics," [1] said Walter Hallstein, Common Market Commission President, to a university audience. In his speech, delivered four years after the founding of the Common Market, Hallstein was attempting to rectify a broad confusion about the character and significance of the institution and was saying as bluntly as he could that the Common Market's paramount interest was not business and economics but politics and the building of a United States of Europe. The political nature of the Common Market was advertised to the world when in 1963 President de Gaulle decided to terminate negotiations for British membership after the British accepted polaris missiles from the United States and refused to join with France in nuclear arms development. The Common Market's quiet political struggle since 1958 to be born and to show some sort of tangible success enabled it to survive the crisis, however. In 1965, another political spasm was caused by a half-year boycott of the Common Market by the French government. The issue was not the price of eggs, but the Common Market constitution—how it worked—because to the French the institution had progressed to the point where it *counted* politically. And they feared that the dosage of curative being administered to the European economy by the Common Market could no longer be determined by the patients—the member nations.

[1] *Economic Integration and Political Unity in Europe* (London: European Community Information Service, 1961, [Community Topics No. 2]). This May 22, 1961, speech was delivered to a combined Harvard-MIT audience.

The Common Market had become an integral part of the political order of Europe both international and national, hence the proper study of all who were interested in European government and politics, or regional international organization. This book is a discussion of the distribution of power within the Common Market and the institution's way of deciding issues and taking action. It does not delve into the technical economic mission of the Common Market nor is it a polemic for European unity. It is a neutral inquiry into the evolving political order of Europe, which takes all relevant material into account, whether it be the formal constitutions, regulations, and court decisions, or the gentlemen's agreements, informal institutional dynamics, or biases of men in positions of power. Gathering information on the politics of the Common Market posed a special problem. Its documentation is very limited, and American political intuitions are not always trustworthy points of departure for analyzing European political phenomena. A Fulbright research grant was of great value, however, in enabling me to visit the dispersed offices of the institution, talk with European civil servants and diplomats, and read documentation unavailable outside the Common Market offices. A Ford Public Affairs grant administered by Carleton College also assisted in the preparation of this book. I am indebted for numerous suggestions from Hans Schmitt, who read a large part of the manuscript at an early stage, and from Leon Lindberg, who read the final product.

W.H.C.

Contents

ix

The New Politics of Europe

1

On July 1, 1965, the Common Market came to an "end." It had existed since the consummation of the marriage of France, Germany, Italy, and the Benelux countries in an economic union effective January 1, 1958, and ended when the French government decided to leave the bed and board of the European Economic Community (the more sedate name of the union). The French complaint was that her marriage partners had been bossy and irreverent of her independence, but amidst the scuffle at departure there was no chance to determine how or when France could be won back. Without France the union was dissolved, because crucial decisions of the union required French agreement. Without French participation, the institution would eventually stop like a clock that had had its last winding. There was talk of seeking a new marriage partner, like Britannia; but, as in the nature of marital spats, the wayward France returned to the union on January 17, 1966, got nowhere with the list of demands she had prepared during her sulking, and appeared content to perpetuate the union after reassurance by the partners that in the future a sharper ear would be bent toward France's interests.

Why did France return? What were the ties that did not snap as the leadership of France tried to sunder the union? What was it that had made a political society of the European Community within the first eight years of its life?

The Phoenician Princess

One may divide the world roughly into regions—say, of Europe, the Middle East, the Far East, Africa, and the Western Hemisphere —but, though such a division is in some ways useful, it is thoroughly misleading insofar as it implies comparable geographic and political integrity for all regions. One need not delve deeply into the question of the comparative integrity of other regions to establish that Europe possesses far more than any of the others. The case of Europe is unique. During the imperial age Europe was the hub around which other nations revolved, and they were oriented to the hub and not to each other. The dependencies that have detached themselves from Europe since 1945 have only begun searching for some basis for unity among themselves. On the other hand, by the time of the ominous rise to nuclear power of the Soviet Union, which lent a decisive note of urgency to European integration in 1949, the unifying process was already well advanced in Europe in numerous respects.

The name of *Europa*—the Phoenician princess whom Zeus in the form of a bull abducted—has been a "geographical expression" since the early middle ages. There were times prior to nationhood when China, India, Germany, and Italy were all geographic expressions, too; but history has shown in their cases that a geographic entity can evolve into a nation. But is nationhood possible for Europe? A glance at a world map of population density reveals four major "islands" of population—China, India, the United States, and Europe—and of these only Europe is not united politically. From this standpoint, Europe is the *last* great population center to be integrating rather than the first region to be integrating; and it is this distinction that separates the case of Europe from that of the American, African, and Asian regions that are struggling for some new order.

Ringed by natural barriers—the permafrost on the North, trackless Siberia on the East, the inland seas on the South, and the Atlantic Ocean on the West—Europe has stood apart from other peoples across thousands of miles of unpopulated or sparsely populated spaces. Its people are nearly all of the white race and thus more homogeneous than the mixed races of India and the United States. All the chief languages of Europe have more in common with one another than they have with any African or Asian language or than the several languages of India or China have with each other. Europe has a common religion and, therefore, more religious unity than China or India; moreover Europe's religion is distinct from those of its neighbors in the Middle East and Asia.

All Europe shares a common tradition in the arts and sciences, which, before the rise of the New World, had no counterpart in another region. The Renaissance and Enlightenment were common to all Europe in varying degrees. The early modern European universities served international student bodies; and, even after the advent of national educational systems in Europe, all the systems had much in common and followed a pattern distinct from that used elsewhere in the world. Plastic arts and, above all, music were the common "language" of Europe and clearly distinct from the folk art and music of neighboring regions. The rapid development of European science, invention, and productivity were phenomena shared throughout the continent; and they created the most conspicuous distinctions between life in Europe and life elsewhere. Unlike the channels of trade that linked American and Asian nations with Europe and not with one another, European trade was heavily intraregional in character, amounting at one time to half of all the international trade of the world.

Possibly the most convincing indication of natural European integrity is the fact that Europe has already known several periods of political unity, from the Roman empire through the empires of Charlemagne, Charles V, Napoleon, and Hitler. But since empires in Europe were created by force of arms, the fact they did not last is just as important as the fact of their having existed. Force had failed—as testify the fifty million souls lost in Europe during the Second World War, who paid the price of Hitler's aspirations for European rule. Despite all its geographic, linguistic, racial, religious, artistic, scientific, and historic bases for unity, Europe refused to unite within a framework debased by the use of force. The end of the Second World War found Europe divided in half by the most inflexible political division of the modern era, the Iron Curtain; and national political life reasserted itself in age-old patterns. Although yesterday's empires in Europe gave a vision of unity tomorrow, they did not show the *way* to union.

The Architecture of Consent

Although Europe had to eschew force as its catalyst for unity, it was not altogether at the mercy of unwilling nationalists. The house of Europe had been more than a century in the building, and the architecture of consent was already taking shape. Ever since Dante's appeal for a universal empire in the fourteenth century, European intellectual history has been dotted with spokesmen for the idea of a united Europe, and in 1834 the first movement for European unity, Young Europe, was founded by Joseph Mazzini, one of the fathers of Italian unity. The movement perished before gaining any wide support, but another cropped up after the First World War, Count Coudenhove-Kalergi's Pan-European Union. This latter movement became the first to have support from government leaders when in 1930 the honorary president of the Union, Aristide Briand, addressed a plan for European unity to the capitals of Europe in his capacity as prime minister of France.

Although during the nineteenth and early twentieth centuries the movement for European unity remained far from its objective, important precedents were being set in the formation of European administrative unions. Starting with the international administration of the Rhine River after the Napoleonic wars, there emerged during the nineteenth century a number of international organizations dealing first with communications problems, then with problems of fair international business practices, problems of trading with the Moslem world, and, finally, problems of international commodity markets. In some cases these organizations were established among European governments exclusively, and in others there were extra-European members, but in all cases—with the exception of the early Pan-American organizations—the focus of concern was Europe. There were two fundamental reasons why early international organization was preeminently European organization. During the nineteenth century, the sovereign nations of Europe ruled the rest of the world, with the exception of the newly independent nations of the Western Hemisphere, which preferred to remain isolated. And the great bulk of the world's international relations were conducted *among* the states of Europe, whether measured in terms of trade, travel, finance, or diplomacy.

The nineteenth century international organizations did not materialize out of idealism for European unity but out of direct material necessity. Considering the increase in traffic, international rivers had to have international administrations. International railroads required international coordination if only to have standardized and interchangeable equipment. Patents had to be internationalized if they were to mean anything at all. Commercial necessity was an integrating force in Europe, but trade and the international organization necessitated by it could not unify Europe all by themselves or they would have done so before now. Governments were able during the nineteenth century to form the requisite international organizations with little or no reference to "politics." That is to say that, until very recently, such organizations did not call into question national power or basic national policy. They were not fought over in parliament or at the polls, and they did not pose the question of European unity squarely. Still, as a result of the organizations of the nineteenth and early twentieth century, the concept of inter-European organization was clearly etched into official European thinking and hence became a part of the edifice of support for European unity.

The decisive turn toward unity resulted from the Second World War, which broke the relative power of Britain, France, and Germany. It made it impossible for the last of the great overseas empires, those of Britain and France, to be maintained and thus largely deprive Britain and France of their special relationships outside Europe and their reasons for independence within Europe. Perhaps equally important, the exhaustion of the European powers affected the character of nationalist thought among their peoples and drained from it much of its arrogance, leaving them with a simple urge to survive and prosper—in a bomb shelter or in a European union, whichever suited the case. The war, too, gave Europe one more common experience comparable to that of the First World War. The relative decline of the individual Western European nations was a result of the Second World War that

Europeans did not like to think about. They preferred to dwell on the rise of the Soviet Union to dominance over Eastern Europe and to military power superior to that of the Western European nations singly or collectively. There were already important forces insinuating ideas of European unity into European politics; but, more than any other single new factor, the Soviet threat welded the unity idea to the central interests and policies of the states of Western Europe.

The first European reaction to Soviet power was the signing of the Brussels treaty. The treaty was reminiscent of the alliances of Europe against the Germany of Hitler and the France of Napoleon in times past; but it embodied organizational patterns only newly experienced by the allies during the world wars, including institutions for the formulation of common policy and international military leadership. The Brussels treaty was a landmark on the way to European unity. It created the first international organization with the constitutional objective of promoting the integration of Europe;[1] and it was, therefore, the first international organization to challenge the nationalist traditions of Europe frontally. The Soviet behavior that had been no more than a matter of prudent public concern in March, 1948, when the Brussels treaty was signed became a genuine war scare by the summer of that year, and popular consent for the fusion of Europe, at least in the military field, could be taken for granted.

But events sped past this issue. The show of Soviet force in toppling the Czechoslovakian government and in blockading the land and water communications between Berlin and the West in 1948 shifted attention to the issue of an American guarantee for Europe. That guarantee was forthcoming in 1949 in the formation of the North Atlantic Treaty Organization (NATO), in which the United States joined the frightened neighbors of the Brussels group in unifying the defenses of the West. And the launching of Communist aggression in Korea in 1950 resulted in a tightening of the NATO alliance.

Winston Churchill had warned Europe that it would have only a brief breathing period after the war during which to build its political household, and now moves toward unity going beyond

[1] Especially Art. 1. Treaty found in *New York Times,* March 18, 1948.

the military field appeared urgent. First the Brussels group established the Council of Europe, which was designed to give an official sounding board to the members of European national parliaments who wished to debate European unity in a permanent and open forum; but such a step had little impact other than to embolden the parliamentarians, whose views the Council helped to publicize, and to provide an instrument for cooperation in certain nonpolitical fields. The Council tried to strengthen its powers, but among the numerous Western European nations that were its members there were always opponents, notably Great Britain, which was still rationalizing its traditional isolation from the continent. Since the whole crowd of nations could not squeeze through the barrier of nationalism together, attempts were made by smaller groups to negotiate passage, and each group took pride in its technique. Belgium, Luxembourg, and the Netherlands had already embarked on their Benelux union, which was predicated upon the efficacy of an economic union with the widest possible mission and a membership of however few nations were up to the effort.

Bold action was taken in the Schuman Plan, promulgated by the 1951 Treaty of Paris as a limited test of European readiness for union, and the test was a success. What the Schuman Plan (the European Coal and Steel Community) entailed was the creation of a common market among France, Germany, Italy, and the Benelux countries only, involving the coal and steel industries only. In material terms, the step was a small one. France and the Benelux countries had relatively self-contained coal and steel industries. And although Germany was going to have to import large quantities of French iron, and Italy, large quantities of German coal, these two relationships could have been smoothed out with little fanfare; but the symbolic importance of the Schuman Plan was exploited to the fullest. It symbolized the termination of Franco-German quarrels, and claims were made that the new coal-and-steel pool would make war between France and Germany henceforth impossible. Equally as impressive, the international commission established to administer the new arrangement was given the elevated title of "High Authority" and invested with unprecedented "supranational" powers. Was this then the embryo of a real federal union? It was made to appear so.

The political significance of the move was difficult to assess, and it was assumed that the nationalists of Europe had accepted the Schuman Plan when, in fact, they had merely not bothered to oppose it, having been duly impressed with the smallness of the material change entailed by the Plan. Had the unity movement hit its stride? And could it now proceed to establish supranational authority of real importance? European statesmen set to work in 1954 to draft a plan for the straightforward unification of Europe in conjunction with a plan for a supranational army called the European Defense Community. EDC would have been directed by a supranational "political community," which would have been, in effect, the United States of Europe in that it would not only have made foreign and defense policy for Europe but also European domestic policy.

EDC had been inspired by the need to rearm and restore to nationhood the Federal Republic of Germany, which was still under occupation, without resurrecting the specter of German aggression. If accession to a United States of Europe was the price Germany had to pay for statehood and the means of self-defense, she was ready to pay it; and the German Bundestag ratified the EDC treaty. The audacity of the plan brought the European nationalists out of hiding, however, and the treaty failed of adoption elsewhere, notably in Britain, which would not have anything to do with the treaty, and in France, whose parliament rejected it. It was necessary, therefore, for the statesmen of Europe to work out a less elaborate arrangement to provide Germany with nationhood and a national army.

Just as the readiness of Europe for unity had been exaggerated in the conception of EDC, so was the reaction of the Europhiles to the failure of EDC extreme. The time was obviously not ripe for political and military union, and so those projects were put aside. But why not go ahead with an economic union—in power, finance, labor, transport, agriculture, trade, industry, and the like? To this end European leaders addressed themselves with utmost caution, excising all trouble-making clauses from their new plan. The international commission that was to administer the new plan was to be called simply *The Commission* rather than High Authority or some such pretentious name. Nowhere was the term supranational used, although clearly supranational powers were to be exercised by the new entity. Logically, the existing European Coal and Steel Community would have been amalgamated into the new organization as a department under the heading of "power" or "transport" or "mining," but this issue was sidestepped. Amalgamation could come later if the proposed economic community was accepted.

Planning for an economic community was nearing fruition in the fall of 1956 when the Suez crisis and Soviet penetration into the politics of the Middle East precipitated an oil crisis for Europe and made the development of new industrial power sources a matter of top political priority. Although any international development of power in Europe would have naturally figured among the responsibilities of the projected economic community, it was feared that the grand plan for the community might fail of adoption. Hence, a separate European Atomic Energy Community (Euratom), whose inception had already been pending for several years, became the main object of concern; and under the stress of the Suez crisis the strongest efforts were bent toward adoption of Euratom.

In Rome on March 25, 1957, a small crowd of citizen supporters of the two communities stood outside in a drizzle and cheered when the Capitoline tower bells pealed the signing of the founding treaties; but the spokesmen of all parties acted glum. German Economics Minister Erhard referred to the Common Market treaty as "economic incest"[2] and complained about its protectionist mechanisms. The other governments expressed fears of harmful competition within the group. But to the credit and immense satisfaction of the leaders for European unity, both of the Rome treaties were subsequently approved by the parliaments of the six Schuman Plan countries. At that time the significance of the new "Common Market" was ambiguous. On the one hand, the Rome Treaty[3] had laid the groundwork for a United States of Europe in that it had created a framework for the determination of European economic and social policies—for the determination, one might say, of all

[2] *New York Times,* March 31, 1957.
[3] Although there were two treaties signed in Rome, the Common Market treaty and the Euratom treaty, the term *Rome Treaty* will in this volume refer always to the Common Market treaty unless otherwise specified.

important European policies except those concerning armed forces, foreign policy, ordinary justice, and local government. On the other hand, the new institution had been undersold in that its voluntary rather than supranational features had been emphasized. And the language of the Rome Treaty, too long and technical for the average citizen and parliamentarian to read and understand, looked more like an elaborate and routine customs convention than a far-reaching new order for Europe. The significance of the Treaty depended entirely upon how seriously the European governments intended to honor it.

It was only after about four years of the Common Market's existence and again under the impulse of a European crisis—the 1961 crisis over the building of the Berlin wall—that remarkable achievements were registered. The institution became by the end of 1961 the center for formulating European antitrust and agricultural policy, thoroughly political fields in any country; and the Rome Treaty came to be taken more seriously by the government of the United Kingdom, which applied for membership and thus threatened to break a tradition of British noninvolvement in continental politics. If New Year 1958 was the birthday of the Common Market in law, New Year 1962 was its birthday in fact; and, as Common Market personnel put it, the Common Market had passed the "point of no return" [4] on the road toward federal Europe. By voluntary steps Europe had acquired a unifying framework more propitious than any previously achieved by force. It was this framework that was tested by the French boycott in 1965 and held firm.

The Constitution of Europe

Everything has a constitution in the sense of having a definable makeup, but a political constitution has a special character in that it is more than a mere description of present politics. It is a body of political norms, not immutable, but in essence the confining framework of politics. Although official language in or concerning the Rome Treaty says nothing about a constitution, the frame-

[4] Speech by European Commission President Hallstein, National Press Club, Washington, D.C., April 11, 1962.

work of the European Community can very rightly have the term constitution applied to it, and it is within this framework and around this framework that the politics of the Common Market unfold.

The institutional pattern of the Common Market did not spring fully elaborated from the pen of a constitution writer. Under the guidance of members of a small group of far-sighted European statesmen, it evolved by stages over the brief span of a decade between the making of the Brussels alliance in 1948 and the inauguration of the Common Market in 1958. The Brussels Treaty organization revolved around a council of ministers, and such a council was central in each of the organizations created thereafter. A new element was introduced when the Council of Europe was created in 1949. European parliamentarians since before the turn of the century had expressed themselves on the problems of their continent through their purely private organization, the Interparliamentary Union. But they now wanted to have their debates and resolutions bear the seal of the Council of Europe. They were given a chamber within the household of the Council, but decision-making power was carefully reserved to the ministers' chamber of the Council.

When the Schuman Plan began in 1952, it had no connection with the earlier creations; but it mimicked their councils of ministers and of parliamentarians. And it introduced two innovations of its own, an executive commission, called the High Authority, and a court to assure that neither the executive nor other parties subject to the Plan would misapply it. The Common Market and Euratom began in 1958 with institutions like the Schuman Plan—ministers, parliamentarians, executives, and court.

Although the Schuman Plan, the Common Market, and Euratom were created separately, they shared the same court and the same parliamentary body. But there were three councils of ministers and three executive commissions. A treaty for the fusion of these superfluous bodies was signed however in 1965 and was to be put into effect when ratified, which would thus yield, for all practical purposes, a single consolidated European Community. By that time, however, the names "Economic Community," "Coal and Steel Community," and "Atomic Energy Community" had still not been eradicated from existing treaties; and so there remained the legal fiction of *three* communities. The fusion occasioned some political feuding, because the French government seized upon the slightest rearrangement of institutions to attempt to shear them of their supranational powers. There were few mechanical problems to be solved, however. The Coal and Steel and Atomic Energy communities formed natural departments of the all-embracing Economic Community and could be accepted into its household with little more difficulty than the moving of a quantity of office furniture and the temporary upsetting of routine.

In short, the Common Market (or "European Community") has four principal organs: (1) the Council of Ministers, composed of a minister from each member government, which enacts the Community's "legislation"; (2) the Commission, composed of persons serving without instructions from member governments although elected by the member governments, which formulates policy proposals and administers the legislation adopted; (3) the European Parliament, composed of parliamentarians chosen by national parliaments, which has the duty to advise the other bodies on Community policy and the power to remove the members of the Commission from office; and (4) the Court of Justice, composed of judges elected by the member governments, whose main function is to void any action of the institutions or member nations that violates a Community regulation or treaty.

History provides no neat counterpart arrangement of political institutions, but there are strong parallels between these Community institutions and the primitive parliamentary democracies that emerged in Europe, starting with the English Parliament as far back as the thirteenth century. The absence of a monarch from the framework of the European Community is an obvious difference, but one can see in the Council of Ministers of the European Community an institution something like the English assemblies of notables—the Curia Regis or the House of Lords—the bodies with whose concurrence important decisions of government could be made. In the Commission of the Community one sees a parallel with the cabinet ministers of the early parliamentary regimes in England, who were charged with policy formulation and execution and with the responsibility to manage as best they could the deliberations of the nearly powerless lower house, the House of Commons. A similarity between the European Parliament and the early English House of Commons exists partly because the European Parliament is only beginning to inch its way toward real power and partly because it is a popular house elected by means other than general suffrage. Thus, for example, in the late thirteenth-century reign of Edward I [5] many new statutes were adopted by the assembly of barons without reference to the Commons just as many Common Market policies are adopted by the Council of Ministers without reference to the European Parliament. The European Parliament, like the Commons of Edward's day, has no meeting place of its own in the household of the Common Market in Brussels, but it must borrow the hall of the Council of Europe in Strasbourg just as the original English Commons had to borrow the Chapter House of the Monks of Westminster in order to discuss in advance the ideas they would present in the throne room that housed the Lords. Although an analogy between these two primitive constitutions has weaknesses, it should impart as general and comprehensible a notion of the constitution of the Common Market as is possible at present. The authors of the European institutions bowed to necessity rather than any particular concept of political form and did not therefore provide those of us who seek to understand the new Europe with any illuminating formula like the analysis of the American constitution given us by its authors in the *Federalist Papers*.

The constitution of the Common Market created several arenas of political activity, and each is the subject of analysis below. There is to be considered, on the one hand, the political behavior of governments and officials *within* each of the political organs and, on the other hand, the struggle *among* the institutions as each one seeks to cultivate its own role in the determination of European policy. Beyond these forms of internal interaction there are relations of the Community with outside powers. This ensemble of relations constitutes the new politics of Europe.

The politics of any institution are often governed by political phenomena not mentioned in its constitution, and informal governors of Common Market behavior will have their full share of

---

[5] Cf. Wm. Stubbs, *The Constitutional History of England*, 3rd ed. Oxford: The Clarendon Press, 1887, vol. II, p. 251ff.

attention in this book, whether they be phenomena peculiar to the Community, such as the role of personality in an international executive, or Europe-wide manifestations of such familiar political forces as political parties, pressure groups, and public opinion.

The Council

II

The Common Market bears out Northcote Parkinson's satiric "law" of administration that the health and vitality of a political institution is shown in the cramped inadequacy of its buildings. The Council of Ministers of the Common Market has used one striking piece of real estate, the new *Palais des Congres*, leased only temporarily and already inadequate. It rests on a commanding height in Brussels that was cleared of some of the most charming but crumbling old European houses and is pierced by a street busy with automobile traffic, the popular symbol of the new Europe. Bedecked with the flags of Belgium, France, Germany, Italy, Luxembourg, and the Netherlands, this building has been the scene every few weeks of meetings of the most powerful and well-known personalities of the European Community institutions, the foreign ministers of "the Six," the member nations of the Community. These men with the raising of their hands can enact legislation binding upon nations encompassing the vast majority of Western Europe's lands and peoples. Provided their enactments are within the sweeping authorities granted by the Rome Treaty, there is no need for ratification by home parliaments or governments nor recourse to higher authority.

15

Lawgiver

The Council was empowered by the Rome Treaty to "ensure the coordination of the general economic policies of the Member States"[1] and was thereby vested with plenary power to make all basic decisions relating to the economic evolution of the Community. But the Treaty by no means stopped there. In more than one hundred pages of other provisions the Council was designated as the decider of a long list of specific questions that the treaty authors could foresee confronting the Common Market. In some fields where foresight was difficult, the Council was empowered to amend the treaty so as to widen its own powers when required by new circumstances. The global power of the Council was conditioned, however, by a variety of formulas stating how the Council must deal with other Common Market organs in its exercise of authority. The most general formula read, ". . . the Council, acting by means of a qualified majority vote *on a proposal of the Commission,* shall decide . . . ,"[2] and thereby the Council was divested in most instances[3] of the power of initiative. The Commission had that power. The "lawmaking" power of the Council naturally gave it a strong, unseen hold over the initiative of the Commission, but the Commission's initiative was intended as a check on the Council.

There were other limitations whose importance promised to grow with time. First, the Council of Ministers was not the chief administrative body in the Common Market as was its counterpart, for instance, in France. There is an unfortunate confusion caused by use of the name Council of Ministers, because in the Common Market the Council is actually a legislative body. The members of the Council may have ministerial responsibilities at home, but at Common Market headquarters they are *lawmakers.* The true "council of ministers" of the Common Market is the so-called Commission, whose functions *are* distantly analogous to those of the

---

[1] Communauté économique européenne, *Traité instituant la Communauté économique européenne et documents annexes.* Bruxelles, 1957, Art. 145.

[2] Cf. idem Arts. 14, 25, 28, etc. Italic emphasis is the author's.

[3] The Council has the initiative in a few specific matters.

Council of Ministers in the government of France. It would be the Commission, therefore, and not the Council of the Common Market that would accumulate the power and prestige involved in implementing Common Market legislation, and the fiercest political battle fought in Brussels has been over the Commission's threat to upstage the Council. Second, the Rome Treaty required the Council to consult *other* bodies on most matters, including the European Parliament, the Economic and Social Committee, and the Monetary Committee; but consultation with these bodies was conceived mainly as an administrative device by which the Council could get professional and political advice. Decision rests exclusively with the Council. The Council has to keep a weather eye on the political implications of its treatment of the Parliament in particular, however, and with the passage of time the influence of the Parliament is destined to grow.

The power and effectiveness of the Council has been enhanced by the fact that the foreign ministers of the continental nations spend a large part of their official lives together on the common business of European defense and economic cooperation. The Council meets about two or three times a month for about two days each time, which occupies about a fifth of the working days of this group—more when business is pressing. Such a commitment of time makes the Common Market one of the absorbing responsibilities of the ministers, and they can keep their minds on their Common Market work.

Besides the frequency of the foreign ministers' meetings, the length of personal involvement of individual members has had a bearing on the evolution of the Council. The first half decade of the Common Market coincided roughly with the tenure of the De Gaulle government in France, the Adenauer government in Germany, the Fanfani government in Italy, the De Quay government in the Netherlands, the Werner government in Luxembourg, and the Lefèvre government in Belgium. The Common Market was managed by a "board of directors" that had been acquainted for a long time with it and with one another, which contributed to the ease and success with which the Council of Ministers operated. It gave the Council a life and personality of its own such as it never could have had otherwise. It was possible for issues to be discussed intelligently over long periods of meetings, because the ministers could recall what had gone on before and where they were headed in the dialogue. The years 1963 to 1965 threatened change with the fall of the Fanfani government in Italy, the resignation of Chancellor Adenauer in Germany, and the resignation of the Lefèvre government in Belgium. Nonetheless, even if there were to be an average of one European governmental change per year or if there were several governments that changed in a given year, the Council's work is likely to be characterized by continuity, which, if ever lost at all, would be lost only temporarily.

Ministers as Sovereigns

In using the term Ministers, the Rome Treaty required only that the members of the Council hold ministerial rank in their national governments and left open the question of what kind of ministers. The Council was composed of foreign ministers by gentleman's agreement, but individual nations did not have to comply. Certain governments wanted foreign ministers in the Council for three main reasons. First, foreign ministers were traditionally the second-ranking minister in European governments; and, since it would have been impractical to compose the Council of prime ministers, the use of foreign ministers placed the Council on as high a political plane as practicable. Second, the foreign ministers were the ministers most preoccupied with the political aspects of international relations; and, since the foremost objective of the Common Market was to take political steps toward a United States of Europe, its direction was best placed in the hands of international politicians. Third, the foreign ministers had interests that were primarily international or outward looking—less keyed to the maelstrom of domestic economic concerns—and were therefore the most congenial overseers of the builders of the house of Europe. They were as apt to represent the interests of the Common Market to their home governments as to represent the interests of their home governments to the Common Market.

Only one government took ideological exception to naming foreign ministers to the Council, and that was the West German government, which placed Common Market affairs under a special branch of its Economics Ministry. From time to time a subordinate minister (state secretary) from the German foreign office sits in the Council, but the German foreign minister rarely attends personally. There have also been some minor departures from the original concept of a council of ministers. The early years of the Common Market were a time of troubles for Belgium—foreign trouble in the Congo and domestic trouble over bilingualism and a sagging coal economy—and so the Belgian foreign minister, who was also the vice premier in a coalition government, almost never attended the Common Market Council. He was, however, represented by an aide, whose near perfect attendance contributed to the continuity of the Council. Although the Italian foreign minister has been active in the Council, Italian representation has been handled for long periods by the commerce minister for personal rather than ideological reasons.

A significant addition to the original concept of the Council has been the convening of specialized groups of ministers, such as the ministers for nuclear energy, for transport, and for agriculture, to exchange views on specialized problems before the Council. As early as 1962 most meetings of the Council were of this type.[4] Such special meetings are treated like ordinary meetings of the Council, operating with the same procedures and the same staff and numbered in series with the foreign ministers' meetings. Although after the first use of the specialized meetings in the Common Market[5] there was some concern expressed over the looseness with which the concept of the Council was being applied, worries were resolved by agreement to confine the specialized meetings to preparatory discussions, leaving the lawmaking decisions to meetings of the foreign ministers or their specially designated substitutes who often sat for them.

[4] For a tabulation of attendance at meetings see P.-H. J. M. Houben, *Les Conseils de Ministres des Communautés Européennes*. Leyden: A. W. Sythoff, 1964, Annex VI.
[5] The Schuman Plan council had had similar experience earlier.

How Sovereignty Is Gained and Lost

Upon arriving in Brussels for sessions of the Council, the ministers go immediately into plenary session with only a minimum of briefing necessary. There is no need to take time for cloakroom politics or cocktail-lounge diplomacy, because all such preliminary conversations have already been carried on by the "permanent representatives" of the member nations in Brussels (as will be explained in the next section). The decision-making process of the Council is almost entirely institutionalized, which contrasts with international organizations like the United Nations whose decisions are often prepared through direct contacts outside the framework of the organization and whose meetings serve only as the means by which decisions are formalized and the views of the delegates registered by the press.

The meetings of the Council are working sessions, the productivity of which is enhanced by the fact that they are closed to the press and to the public, as are the meetings of the permanent representatives. Minutes are kept, but none of these are shown to the press, and the most confidential debates are also withheld from the version mimeographed for internal use within the Common Market.

The atmosphere of the meetings of the Council is something less than intimate, and there could be little intimacy lost in case new members should be admitted to the Common Market. The six-nation Council meets in a room larger than that used by the nine-member Commission, and the chairs around the immense conference table are filled with from one to four delegates from each nation. The technical character of the Council's agenda necessitates the rotation of specialized delegates in some instances, and the delegates are accompanied by their permanent representatives and other aides either from the permanent Brussels offices or from home ministries. The Council tried to limit the attendance of advisers to three per delegation but had to yield to pressures against the limit, raising it to five. At least one and sometimes all the members of the Commission are present, also with necessary aides. This brings the total around the table to about forty or fifty, depending upon the agenda. The work of the Council would be clumsier still if new nations were admitted to its circle. The Council expedites sensitive business occasionally, however, by meeting in what it calls a *cadre restreint:* a small room with only the Commission, the Council, and its secretary (who keeps no verbatim records) present.

Such a body is as much in need of rules of procedure as councils of the United Nations, and there appears to be little hope of simplifying these sessions. The Rome Treaty required the Council to adopt rules of procedure and it did adopt provisional rules[6] during its first year, but the key rules were laid down in the Treaty itself. The Treaty stipulated that the delegates were to serve six-month terms as president of the Council in the alphabetical order of the names of their countries: Belgique (Belgie), Bundesrepublik Deutschlands, France, Italia, Luxembourg, Nederland. More important, the Treaty was very detailed as to the Council's voting system—so explicit that it would have to be entirely rewritten in case any additional nation or nations joined the Common Market. The member states were named in the Treaty, and the number of votes necessary to pass certain measures were set out in specific figures rather than in general principle.

There are four voting formulas. The Treaty required the Council to decide all matters by simple majority vote unless otherwise specified, but this provision meant in effect that only procedural and administrative decisions were to be taken by simple majority, because special voting formulas were stipulated by the Treaty for all the substantive issues to be decided by the Council. There are sixty-five[7] different types of decisions[8] the Council has to make by unanimous vote, a more stringent voting formula than that applied in the Security Council of the United Nations; and invariably the decisions requiring unanimity are the most important ones. Admittedly, the unanimity rule gives strong protection to national interests in the Council, but the Council is no ordinary diplomatic con-

---

[6] Not as yet in final form or published in the *Official Journal,* but the provisional rules can be found in Houben, *op. cit.,* Annex V.

[7] Numbers are based on tabulation by Leon Lindberg, *The Political Dynamics of European Economic Integration.* Stanford, Calif.: Stanford University Press, 1963, pp. 229-307.

[8] "Decisions" is used here to refer to *all* forms of action taken by the Council. The Rome Treaty used a wide vocabulary of synonyms to denote various types of actions.

ference. Its decisions are directly binding on member nations without need of any ratification by a parliament or head of state. One might interpret this unanimity formula as a way for the sovereign states of Europe to cast away bits of sovereignty while meeting in a framework that does not in itself limit sovereignty.

Although the most fundamental decisions were to be made by unanimous vote indefinitely, there were two categories of unanimous decisions that were scheduled by the Treaty to change with time. That is to say, six types of these unanimous decisions were, after the first four-year stage of the Common Market, to be made by a *qualified majority,* and another six types were to be made by qualified-majority vote after the end of the second four-year stage. One further type of decision would become majoritarian at the end of the twelve-year transition period. Hence, within twelve years the number of types of decisions requiring unanimity was to shrink from sixty-five to fifty-two.

The qualified majority was an important concept of the Treaty, and from the outset forty-six types of decisions could be taken in this way. The thirteen types of decisions that would shift from the unanimous to the qualified-majority voting formula would swell the number to fifty-nine. When making qualified-majority decisions the votes of the member nations were weighted, with the three great powers, France, Germany, and Italy, each getting four votes; Belgium and the Netherlands, two each; and Luxembourg, one. Thus there were a total of seventeen votes; the qualified majority necessary was twelve. Any twelve votes would do if the Commission sponsored the text being voted on, but, if the text did not come from the Commission, the twelve votes had to include at least four member governments.

One gets a clearer concept of what qualified-majority voting means if one regards it as qualified unanimity. In essence, it is a formula by which no one nation, even if a great power, can defeat a proposal alone. If any one great power were to vote "no" with the support of any other power except Luxembourg, on the other hand, it *could* defeat a measure. Hence, the qualified majority puts aside the great-power veto. The provision that at least four nations have to vote "yes" on any text not originating from the Commission is simply a way of saying that at least one Benelux member has to concur in the decision (e.g., France four, Germany four, Belgium two, and the Netherlands two totals four nations and twelve votes). The requirement of four concurring nations can effectively raise the total votes needed to more than twelve (e.g., France four, Germany four, Italy four, and the Netherlands two total four nations and fourteen votes).

As the Common Market has approached maturity, the qualified majority scheme has become increasingly a determining factor in the character and achievement of the Community. Although a qualified majority is only a short step away from the traditional diplomatic practice of unanimous voting, it signalizes more than anything else the positive transfer of sovereignty in economic questions from the European nations to the European Community. *Any European member nation, large or small, could be bound without its consent under the qualified-majority formula.* Also, there is a safety factor in the majority principle that prevents strong economic interests, such as the European auto manufacturers, from ganging up on one government and bribing it to veto some undesired measure.

The Rome Treaty enumerated a long list of mandates for the Council and allowed it only the latitude to modify or delay proposals formulated by the Commission. The Council is free to reject any proposal of the Commission, but its mandates could scarcely be fulfilled if it should make a regular practice of rejection. Hence, normally, action in the Council results in the adoption of a measure *in hand* or its postponement. There are so few voting members that a deep division over an issue does not need to be tested by formal vote, and proposals contested by more than one member in the Council are immediately slated for review by the permanent representatives of the member governments in Brussels. When there are no objections, the mechanics of voting are simple. The president merely states there is unanimity without taking an actual vote and passes on to the next issue.

Differences are inevitable, however, and formal votes are sometimes taken. There are no political parties in the Council, and so the lines of opposition are drawn differently on different issues. Despite the existence of the Benelux customs union, for instance, the Belgian, Dutch, and Luxembourgian delegations do not act as a bloc in the Council. The Treaty gave the Benelux countries an exaggerated voting strength—they have five votes to Germany's four despite the fact that they have only half as large a population as Germany. But just in case they do vote together in the negative, as they have in fact done, they fall just short of enough votes to defeat a measure proposed by the Commission. They can prevent adoption of a measure *not* proposed by the Commission, however. The term *Bonn-Paris axis* is used popularly to point out the dominant positions of France and Germany in the Common Market, but these two do not form any sort of bloc either. They frequently stand on opposite sides of an issue. The Treaty provided that a Council member could act as proxy for another member, but the proxies are not for the use of "party leaders" as had been true in the French parliament. In fact, proxies have been cast on one side of an issue by nations that have voted on the other side themselves. The proxy concept was intended to compensate for delegates' absences from meetings, and they have been absent a third of the time, on the average.[9] The Council has no quorum requirement.

Despite the theoretical advance in international voting procedure represented by the Council's majority voting formulas, there is still a tendency in the Council to seek unanimity and avoid closely chiseled majority decisions. Once, for instance, while voting on an appropriation measure, the German delegate said he would approve if the other delegates did. The Treaty required only a qualified majority for such decisions, but the German delegate would go along only on the basis of unanimity. The next vote was cast by France, whose delegate opposed the appropriation, which, with the German negative vote, would have killed the measure. But, to enable the measure to pass, another vote was taken, and this second time the French delegate abstained, which enabled the German delegate to join in a unanimous vote. Abstentions in the Council do not necessarily count as no votes.

The key test of the voting regime of the Common Market was the Council's willingness actually to take by majority vote those decisions the Treaty allowed it to. It was one thing for the Treaty to define a broad category of decisions that could be taken by ma-

[9] Houben, *op. cit.*, p. 129. The Schuman Plan council members were absent two-thirds of the time.

jority vote and quite another for the Council to force a majority decision down the throat of one recalcitrant delegate. The first crisis over the majority voting principle occurred in June, 1965, when the capacity of the Common Market to adopt a policy over the opposition of the French government was put on trial. It was a general trial of principle, and France raised her objection to the majority voting rule to make sure that that rule would succumb expressly if France won her case. The rupture came at a point in the Council's work when the measure at issue was in fact subject to the unanimity rule.

The other Common Market members, with the willing assistance of the Commission, had tried to coerce French agreement to a strengthening of the Common Market with an offer of money the French would find difficult to refuse. What they wanted was French agreement to assign a limited amount of direct revenue to the Community, as envisaged by the Treaty, and to strengthen the budgetary powers of the European Parliament. They intended to make agreement worthwhile by consenting at the same time to pay the vast agricultural subsidies to France that were called for by the Community's agricultural plan.

The French government registered its opposition to the scheme as soon as it was unveiled in March, 1965; but the partisans of the scheme held out. They possibly counted on pressure from French agricultural interests to prevent the De Gaulle government from blocking the measure. But De Gaulle still had a trump card. The French delegate said neither yes nor no, waited until the end of the timetable for agreement on the issue (June 30), and walked out, blaming the others for *their* failure to agree to the subsidies. The others came back after a few weeks with a scheme of the sort France had asked for, but the French decided to continue sulking throughout the fall of 1965, their election period, during which President de Gaulle was elected for a second seven-year term by a small popular majority. When in January, 1966, the French foreign minister returned to the Council, an icy reception by the patient five ruled out the possibility of their accepting a French demand for universalizing the unanimity rule; but the Council went on record as deeming majority voting a "last resort" if attempts to achieve unanimity should prove fruitless. This declaration did not amount to a change in the behavior of the Council; it merely brought that behavior out into the open. But, in doing so, it tended to perpetuate the habitual avoidance of majority decision making.

The Council's Council

What had kindled early resentment among the French was that they had been unable to block the financing proposal before it came out in the open and was placed before the Council where the nature of French opposition could not be masked. The French refused to be outmaneuvered in this way and chose to boycott rather than veto. The key to the trouble was the fact that the Council did not do all of its own work but often only completed actions that had been painstakingly prepared in advance of their meetings by consultations and meetings of the permanent representatives of the member governments. It is here that one must look to find the spark that lit the fiery reaction.

As agreed at the time of the negotiation of the Rome Treaty, each government established a mission to the Common Market in Brussels headed by a permanent representative of ambassadorial rank. At first these representatives aided the Councils on only an *ad hoc* basis, but with the passage of time their work became increasingly routinized and elaborated. By the end of five years the permanent delegations of the great powers—France, Germany, and Italy—numbered between forty and fifty officers each, plus clerical help, and included specialists in every area dealt with by the Common Market. The three lesser members had delegations of proportionately smaller size, not being able to afford as high a degree of specialization of functions.

The place of permanent representatives in the decision-making process of the Council was largely determined by experience with a similar preparatory body under the Schuman Plan. Policy initiative is generally the prerogative of the Commission, the executive body of the Common Market; and, when that body prepares a draft for enactment by the Council, it discusses it first of all with the administrative officers most concerned in the capitals of the member governments, who then informally pass on the details of the proposals to the permanent representatives in Brussels for their information. The Commission is not *obliged* to act on criticism from the national administrations, although some ministries such as the French ministry of overseas territories have been the font of much Commission policy. And it is here that the Gaullist government demanded a stronger national voice, possibly national initiative to present its own draft policies instead of the drafts from the Commission. At the first meeting of the Council thereafter the proposal is introduced for referral *pro forma* to the permanent representatives and is produced as a Council of Ministers document. At this point there is no certainty about when the proposal will emerge for final adoption by the Council; proposals on which agreement is not forthcoming are remanded repeatedly to the permanent representatives by the Council for further efforts toward compromise. Several important issues, therefore, might be faced simultaneously by the permanent representatives over an extended period. Their work load has been lessened somewhat by the creation of certain specialized preparatory groups, such as the Council's Special Committee on Agriculture, that work parallel with them.

The permanent representatives hold meetings one day per week, leaving the four other workings days free for study of proposals by their own working groups, which specialize in social, transport, agricultural, tariff, commercial, and other questions. All six governments are represented in all working groups, and specialized personnel may be brought in to discuss each different proposal. In the smaller delegations a single permanent staff member may have to serve on several working groups, however, as in Luxembourg's, which has had fewer permanent staff members than there are working groups. The volume of reports from working groups has become too great for consideration by the permanent representatives themselves, and so they have empowered their deputies to serve as negotiators in their place on less contentious proposals. The deputies and permanent representatives cannot hold meetings simultaneously, however, because the deputies have to be prepared to take the places of the permanent representatives should the latter be unable to attend a meeting. Two permanent representatives that participated in the negotiations for British membership in the

Common Market, for example, were often unable to attend meetings and had to be replaced there by their deputies.

Since the permanent representatives carry such great responsibility, the Commission has to launch its campaign for adoption of proposals among *them*. This became especially important after 1961 when the Council decided as a matter of principle to refer as many issues as possible for preliminary decision in meetings of the permanent representatives. The Commission meets the day before the permanent representatives' meetings to plan their latest moves in what often proves to be a long dialogue between the representatives and the Commission as week by week painful compromises are worked out. The secretary-general of the Commission's private staff attends all the meetings of the permanent representatives to speak for the Commission, and he is assisted by technical personnel from Commission headquarters if the intricacy of the issue at hand warrants it.

The permanent representatives base their treatment of an issue on the report of the appropriate working group; but, if a working group requires an extended period of time, it submits monthly progress reports to the permanent representatives which also serve as progress reports to the Council. As a meeting of the Council approaches, the permanent representatives make up an agenda consisting of issues that have already been resolved by them, designated with the letter A, and issues that remain unresolved, marked B. This technique was borrowed from Belgian and French governmental practice.[10] In February of 1962, for example, after a long period of examination at all levels, a proposal for the association of the Netherlands Antilles with the Common Market finally came up for Council decision marked A and was therefore adopted by the Council perfunctorily, albeit before that time there had been a hot and important controversy over the prospect that the oil refining capacity of the Antilles could upset petroleum pricing in Europe. At the same time, rifts between governments over the proposed association of Turkey with the Common Market caused that matter to be marked B on the agenda. It reached the A agenda in 1963.

It is the B items therefore that are the real problems for the

[10] Houben, *op. cit.*, p. 134.

Council. Respecting some B items, the Council might wish merely to hold an exchange of views to register its reaction to some preparatory work as yet unfinished by the permanent representatives. Sometimes the permanent representatives have reached agreement on all but a few points, being prevented from proceeding further by the instructions of their home governments, and it is possible that a debate in the Council can solve the problem. The foreign ministers might be able to take new positions; make trades with other governments; or, in the case of an isolated government, simply give in on a point agreed to by all the others. It is the cutting of these Gordian knots that is the contribution *par excellence* of the ministers to the work of the whole fabric of Community institutions.

Since the Council is the real decision maker, the Commission hesitates to yield points in its draft proposals in meetings of the permanent representatives, hoping for a more favorable treatment from the Council itself. Hence, an impasse solved by the Council is as apt to be one between the Commission and the permanent representatives as one between governments. Here again the French government felt insufficient weight was being given to national objections.

Sometimes a government insists that an issue be placed on the agenda as a B item even though there is no likelihood of progress on it either in the Council or the meetings of the permanent representatives. The Dutch government, for instance, kept bringing up the issue of the formation of a political union, but the issue was so politically volatile that for years, at any given meeting when it was discussed, there was little or no concrete change in the situation. Likewise the German government often requested the Council to discuss the association of Turkey with the Community, but, until certain changes in Turkish policy paved the way for association in 1963, there was no hope of agreement in the Council. Such issues are taken up by the Council for courtesy's sake but are speedily dealt with, with the minister of the interested nation possibly making the only statement.

The permanent representatives serve as advisers in Council meetings or, on rare occasions, as substitutes for the ministers themselves. Although the same ministers come to Brussels month after month, they still have to rely heavily on their permanent representatives. Possibly the best attendance record of any foreign minister at Council meetings has been that of the French Foreign Minister Maurice Couve de Murville. Still, his permanent representative has been his *alter ego* at Council meetings, advising him at every step of the proceedings. The president of the permanent representatives coincides in nationality with the semiannually rotated presidency of the Council, which makes each president of the permanent representatives for six months one of the most powerful men in the Common Market. Not only does he manage the business of the permanent representatives but also indirectly that of the Council because of the dependence of his compatriot, the president of the Council, upon him.

The bias of the permanent representatives is conditioned by their working continually with one another and with representatives of the Commission; and since their work is, in essence, the Common Market in action, their judgment is strongly affected by the interests of the European community as a whole. Moreover, the first group of permanent representatives spent four years—the entire first stage of the Common Market—at their posts in Brussels so that their attachment to the interests of the Common Market had an especially long period to develop. The usual European diplomatic tour of duty has been only three years.

The permanent representatives are a two-way channel of influence. On the one hand, they represent the positions of their governments to the Community, and, on the other hand, they plead the case of the Common Market to their home governments and are generally as communitarian as the Commission, at least in this respect. The reward for their communitarianism has been clear. When the German and French permanent representatives were first replaced, they were elevated to the rank of secretary of state in their respective foreign ministries. The Italian permanent representative was promoted to secretary-general of the Italian foreign ministry.

Besides the preparatory work of the permanent representatives, the Council has the assistance of its own secretariat. In this respect it is like the Congress of the United States or the parliament of a European government, which has its own staff apart from the executive or administrative agencies of government. The Council's secretariat numbers more than one hundred, and it prepares the meeting facilities and documentation for the Council and its subsidiary bodies. It also handles the Council's official correspondence and relations with the press and other mass media. Its leadership and personnel were inherited from the secretariat of the Schuman Plan council in 1958. With rapidly augmenting numbers they centered their activity in Brussels but maintained meeting facilities in Luxembourg, where, under the terms of the treaty for fusion of the three European communities, the Council was expected to hold its meetings three months per year (about one-third of the working year). The periodic sojourns to Luxembourg were one of that country's demands in connection with the fusion, and for this compromise the circuit-riding secretariat of the Council must pay a price in lost efficiency and dissatisfaction of personnel.

The European Parliament and the executive Commission have been hostile to the Council's reliance on its permanent representatives and secretariat, and once the Parliament recommended unsuccessfully that the secretariat's budget be reduced by one symbolic franc. From the point of view of the Europhile, the embellishment of the nationalistic Council constitutes an obstacle to the growth of power of the internationally minded Commission in that every preparatory or housekeeping function performed by the Council's own household reduces its reliance on the Commission. This doctrinaire opposition springs from mistrust of the national interests represented in the Council and is heedless of the fact that, if it were completely successful, it might cripple the Council, the very institution upon which the achievement of an integrated European economy has depended.

There is little cause for alarm, because throughout its history the Council has never stepped beyond the bounds of its policy-reviewing role. So long as the Council does not preempt the initiative, as the French government unsuccessfully proposed it should in January, 1966, there is no more reason to object to the three hundred or so servants of the household of the Council (including permanent delegations) than to object to the committees of the United States Congress and their staffs. The Parliament's criticisms, moreover, have to be interpreted in the light of the fact that it has been cut off from the exercise of real power. Its resolutions aiming to fight nationalism in the Council have had to be repetitious and dramatic to be influential.

Everyman's Political Who's Who

Criticisms of the Council have tended to obscure its essential position in the movement for European union. *The Council has done more to unify Europe than any other institution in the history of the Continent.* It has had the power to do so, and no other institution has. All the successes of the Common Market have actually been successes of the Council, with the exception of the limited policy areas in which the Commission could act alone. The Council has power because its members represent governments that can make choices, spend vast sums of money, and implement policies. The Parliament attempted to propagate the idea that in becoming a member of the Council, a foreign minister transformed himself into an officer of the Community with identity distinct from his national government, hence he ought to perform all his duties in the Council personally, not through substitute representatives. This notion committed the fallacy of presuming that the power of the Council resides in its members and not in the governments they represent. If the members of the Council were in fact ever to separate themselves from their governments over matters of policy, the Council would promptly become powerless for want of any means to implement its decisions. It was fanciful to even think of such a separation.

Since the Parliament, echoed by the Commission, needled the Council primarily to counteract nationalism, it was the nationalistic French leaders who reacted most hotly to criticism of the Council. In their own self-defense they liked to point out that others of the Six had national interests that were sacrosanct too and that the French only appeared to be most nationalistic because they were apt to be the first to say no. The French are no more nationalistic, they claimed, only more *openly* nationalistic. The French were arguing like the man who was the first to turn off the hot water in a communal bathtub. "None of us in the tub wanted the water to get too hot," the man said, "and so I was serving the interests of all in turning off the hot water." It was clear to all, however, that they could have stood water a little hotter, just as it was clear to the other five members of the Common Market that they could accept stronger Community measures than could Gaullist France. Much has hinged, therefore, on the careful nurturing of the French delegation, since the Rome Treaty offers such generous opportunities for individual governments to block Community action. One of the tonics that appeared to help was to give credit to France for initiating steps she had finally accepted after opposing for a long time. France had blocked the fusion of the European community for years, but was pleased to "propose" the fusion treaty after reversing her position.

President de Gaulle has distinguished himself by his speeches of adulation for nationalism. The defense of national interests by other nations in the Council, however, has tended to be concealed by the secrecy of the Council's operation, particularly the secrecy surrounding its voting. The Council wants secret voting to avoid outside influence as much as possible, and there are powerful interests that could make use of voting information. Vested commercial interests could see whether their governments were backing them in Brussels. National parliaments could see how their governments were represented on Common Market issues. The European Parliament would know whom to blame for the defeat of a measure. The teeth of all these potential detractors are drawn by suppressing voting records. Even the Commission, which is present in the Council when votes are taken, cannot divulge the information—a situation the Commission laments because it could make good use of publicity on certain votes in the Council in order to embarrass governments that oppose their initiatives.

The success of the Common Market, on the other hand, is bound up with Council secrecy in that secrecy enables a no vote today to be converted to a yes vote tomorrow without bringing national pride into the picture. While the plan of association between the Common Market and its members' former colonies was being formulated by the Council in 1960, for instance, numerous reservations about proposed terms were expressed by members of the Council, but one by one they were dropped in the interest of agreement. The Dutch delegate in particular held out for a change, but, since the measure required a unanimous vote, he too came around.

The Council has the interests of the Community at heart, but there is nothing artificial about the Council's communitarianism. It operates within the realities of European politics always. Examples are numerous. When the antitrust law of the Community was being passed by the Council, there were fundamental national differences of approach between Germany, Italy, and the Netherlands on the one hand and Belgium, France, and Luxembourg on the other. When the first regulations to eliminate discriminatory national freight rates was passed, there was immovable Dutch and Italian resistance to certain clauses. Germany and Italy clashed over the terms of a regulation providing for the free movement of laborers in the Common Market that would affect Germany's decision on whether to import Italian or Spanish surplus laborers. In some instances hot words were exchanged, especially when a single nation had been isolated in a position to which it was inflexibly bound, and its delegate was tired of being badgered by the other five. And, too, when a nation's prestige was at stake, a Council measure could suffer, as when the French delegate objected to conferring ambassadorial status upon Common Market agents abroad, which would make them equal in rank to national embassies.

Generally, when there is a clash of national interests, the resulting decision is the lowest common denominator of the delegates' positions. The compromise antitrust law was a weakened measure. The agricultural policy was adopted at first as little more than a group of timetables for the writing of regulations. The regulation on the free international movement of laborers was shorn of problematic provisions concerning the right of laborers to join and lead labor unions and the duty of employers to prefer Common Market surplus labor in hiring. *Unilateral* reservations were made by the delegates as new measures were adopted, which limited their effectiveness.

Fortunately, the task of adjusting national interests was facilitated by the *interchangeability* of interests. For example, Italy was willing to yield its interest concerning the association of Greece with the Common Market—Greek and Italian products are broadly competitive—provided she could be rewarded later by Council decisions favoring the Italian economy. Just how the Council planned to repay the Italians was not specified; and once, when the Italian delegates asked the Council to make good its promise by granting Italy a protective tariff for its leaf tobacco, the Council sidetracked that request but granted Italy a tariff break on aluminum. Luxembourg let the Schuman Plan headquarters be assigned to Brussels as part of the fusion of the communities in exchange for the establishment of certain other Community bureaus in Luxembourg.

Although there are no permanent alignments in the Council, it is possible to identify certain gross characteristics of its political lineup. The Bonn-Paris axis has been a favorite cliché of journalists, despite the insistence of the French and German authorities that they were guilty of neither collusion nor domination. The Dutch Foreign Minister, Mr. Luns, lucidly described the special position of the big two in saying that, when they were "throwing dishes at one another," [11] the others were bound to get hurt; and, when the two were in agreement, it was difficult for the others to stand in their way. The Common Market has revolved around the Bonn-Paris axis regardless of how Bonn and Paris regarded one another.

There has been a typical pattern of Bonn-Paris relations in the Common Market. Discussion of an issue was apt to begin with Bonn taking exception to some French regulatory concept, and Germany would be supported by the three libertarian Benelux members. Germany and the Low Countries have been the most outward-looking Common Market members because they trade so much with nonmember countries such as America, Great Britain, and Scandinavia. A Bonn-Paris struggle over external trade barriers and internal trade integration would progress to the point where Germany considered it had achieved all it could expect from negotiations with France, and then it would come to terms, dragging the Benelux members with it. Holland, being small and even more outward looking than Germany, was apt to be the member most wrenched in this process, and the Dutch representatives became legendary in their ability to resist this fate—demanding frequently that talks be suspended to allow for consultations in the Hague.[12] During an initial period of Bonn-Paris difference over a new issue, the Belgian

[11] Quoted in Robert Lemaignen, *L'Europe au Berceau*. Paris: Plom, 1964, p. 92.

[12] Lindberg, *op. cit.*, p. 82.

representation was apt to serve as the lubricator or matchmaker between clashing forces.

A few examples will place these political relationships in focus. One of the first choices the Common Market had to make was whether it was going to hide behind a tariff wall and engage in what the then German Economics Minister Erhard called "economic incest" or whether it was going to adopt a liberal trade policy toward the outside world. Germany and the Low Countries were the low-tariff countries of the group; they had active trade with non-Common-Market countries. France and Italy, on the other hand, were high-tariff countries, and they looked forward to improving their trade primarily within the Common Market. Negotiations were opened between the Common Market members and the other nations of Europe to examine the possibility of establishing an all-European free trade area and thus let the nonmember countries through the Community's tariff wall. France and Italy opposed the free trade area, while Germany and the Low Countries feared that without free trade their commerce with the outside world would be hampered, possibly to the point of necessitating their *withdrawal* from the Common Market. In the end Germany came around, the Netherlands grudgingly followed suit, and the free-trade-area negotiations misfired.

Afterwards, the French and Italians showed enthusiasm for an acceleration of tariff reductions among Common Market countries ahead of the timetable laid down in the Rome Treaty. Here again Germany and the Low Countries resisted on the grounds that to accent internal trade within the Common Market by too fast a reduction in duties would make it all the harder to retain their stake in trade outside the Community; and, as a condition of acceleration, they demanded that it be accompanied by a drop of twenty per cent in the external tariff of the Community. France and Italy, however, opposed making an unqualified external tariff cut. The Belgians here played their mediating role by proposing that the external tariff cuts be granted to foreign nations on the basis of reciprocity. On this basis, the Germans were willing to come around, followed again by the Dutch, and the Council was able to agree on acceleration.

The outward- versus inward-looking pattern of Council politics related more to manufactures than to food, concerning which some of the roles of governments were reversed. A "seventh member" of the Council, the European Commission, entered the pattern of agricultural politics. The farm problem entailed not merely an adjustment of national interests to one another but the inauguration of an entirely new trading system based on a proposal by the Commission. The new system was necessary because there was no real prospect of adjusting French agriculture to the German trading pattern or vice versa. Thus the initial struggle was over the question of whether the new system would provide the safeguards demanded by member nations—guaranteed internal markets, protection from food from outside the Community, access to one another's markets, and compensation for displaced farmers. The basic trial of strength within this more complicated picture came, as in other matters, between France and Germany. The French sought markets in Europe for their food production, the largest of the Six, and wanted subsidies to support them in competition with other producers in the world market, all within the relatively low price structure to which the French were accustomed. Germany, on the other hand, was subsidizing her farmers, who were less efficient than the French. German prices were relatively high, and the government was hesitant to undergo the internal political spasm that might be caused by too radical a drop in prices.

The Dutch government gave full backing to the Dutch member of the Commission, Sicco Mansholt, who was the sponsor of the new agricultural plan. And soon all the members accepted the Mansholt plan except Germany, which made agreement on the plan a matter of wearing down German resistance. The eventual decision of the German government to change its mind, to accept a low-price unified agricultural market, and to turn energetically to retrain and reintegrate into its economy the inefficient farmers who were displaced by foreign competition, was one of the most statesmanlike acts of the Common Market era. German manufacturers had prospered within the Common Market, but it was impossible to make that sound gratifying to the German farmers who had to bear the brunt of the choice.

Breaking through the biggest obstacle to a common agricultural market was only the first of many problems that had to be solved.

The subordinate decisions concerning the whole range of foods, item by item, took five years to negotiate, and the positions of members varied considerably depending upon where commodities were grown and what the market conditions were for each commodity. Here politics were shapeless; and, from the point of view of the Common Market, shapeless politics were healthy politics. They were neither nationalistic nor doctrinaire.

After 1963, the French rather than the Germans tended to be isolated in the Council, chiefly in connection with constitutional issues concerning which the French assumed a stiff, conservative position. French isolation began over the negotiations for British admission to the Common Market, during which the French found the British terms for joining too much at variance with the French concept of the Community and broke off the negotiations. Only Belgium, the mediator government in the Council, showed sympathy for the French. Similarly the French blocked proposals for enlarging the power of the European Parliament and for vesting revenue and financial power in the European Community. The notoriety these "vetoes" gave France tended to mark it as the bane of the Community; but who could say what nation the cycle of changing issues would isolate next in the Council?

The Commission

III

Out of the ministerial or comparable ranks of the governments of the Six have stepped a few men who hold their heads a bit higher than before, the members of the executive Commission of the Common Market. Their bearing is partly a reflection of their actual prestige, which among the international servants of the world is second only to that of the chief United Nations officials. But it is also a reflection of what they expected themselves or their successors to *become,* the ministers and responsible administrators for the future United States of Europe. Their behavior infuriates the nationalists of Europe, because their every step is inspired by their expectation of future European unity. They are not heading an *experimental* administration that might lead someday to the establishment of a sovereign administration for all Europe. They are constructing the *actual* administration for a European union with civil servants who might, within their professional lives, serve an all-European government.

During the early years of its existence, the Commission inhabited less-than-regal quarters in Brussels, boxlike modern buildings like a good deal of new urban building in Europe. Growing into its work, the Commission leased one massive new structure after another, which came to house as large a headquarters secretariat as that of the United Nations, all with the understanding that this is only a temporary headquarters pending the choice of a capital for Europe. As each new structure rose, expectations were voiced that *it* would house the Commission only to be silenced by the discovery each time that the cloth had been cut too narrow.

The Power of Initiative

The Commission and its agencies are central to the Community for basically the same reason that national cabinets are central to their governments. The Commission is the nexus of all Community activity, providing the administrative comprehensiveness and continuity that hold the fabric of Community institutions together. Unlike national cabinet ministers, however, individual commissioners lack powers in their own right such as might be exercised by a minister of education heading a school system or a minister of transport heading some nationalized railroad. The Commission can act only as a body, but in that framework, at least, it has some real power.

The word *power* (singular) is happier than the word *powers* (plural) in characterizing the Commission in that it does not have a list of law-making authorities as the Council of Ministers has. There are a few provisions of the Treaty that the Commission can implement by itself,[1] but none of these are nearly so significant as the influence the Commission exercises over the Council. Influence is assured by the fact that the Commission can promote its own case, using its vast facilities for research and consultation, and by the fact that, except for a few initiatives reserved to the Council, *policy proposals can originate from no source other than the Commission.*[2] Since the Council can reject a proposal by the Commission, it is plain that the power of initiative in and of itself cannot make the European executive as powerful in *its* household as national cabinets are within theirs.

The chief means by which the Commission can enlarge its power is by accumulating new *administrative* responsibility, by becoming, in other words, a "big government." And a start was made under

[1] These are listed methodically in Leon Lindberg, *The Political Dynamics of European Economic Integration.* Stanford, Calif.: Stanford University Press, 1963, pp. 307-310.

[2] The exceptions are listed in *ibid.*, pp. 299-302.

the Common Market agricultural regulations, which entailed extensive implementation by the Commission. Every time the Commission received bits of authority by vote of the Council—to determine food prices or pass on national demands for tariff breaks—it was a one-way proposition. The stringent voting formulas in the Council promised to hamper any effort to rescind powers of the Commission or overturn any decisions made by the Commission. One or two friends in the Council were all the Commission needed.

The Commission had a battle just exercising its power of initiative, because each new proposal ruffled the nerves of certain national administrators who silently hoped the Rome Treaty would not be followed to the letter. At the beginning of the Common Market it came as a shock to the national agricultural ministries that the Community would actually begin study and discussion of a common agricultural policy, as it did at the Stresa conference convened in 1958.[3] The hazards of initiative were further demonstrated in 1965 when the proposal that the Community collect revenue of its own precipitated the French boycott of that year and the French demand that the power of initiative be curbed. Article 201 of the Rome Treaty authorized the revenue proposal, but it was politically tabu. Since the French government could not get any other member to agree to limiting initiative, it agreed to end its boycott after face-saving assurances were given that French officials would be more closely consulted in the preparation of future proposals. But the rules were not changed.

Civil Servants As Politicians

The household of the Commission was set up on the model of a national administration with only the names changed. At the top is the "prime minister," the President of the Commission, who heads the organization's housekeeping agencies for personnel, budgeting, and administration. Thus, indirectly, he supervises all of the other offices, among which are divided the responsibilities of government as if they were national ministries. The subdivisions

[3] Robert Lemaignen, *L'Europe au Berceau.* Paris: Plom, 1964, p. 163.

are called *directions*, in French, because they are headed by directors; but they would be called departments in English. They are numbered from one to eight, but they correspond in responsibilities to national ministries of foreign relations, finance, interstate commerce, antitrust enforcement, welfare, agriculture, transport, and foreign aid. Each of these is supervised by one of the eight remaining commissioners, who are, in effect, "minister" of foreign affairs, or finance, etc. Terms last four years and can be renewed.

The Council has the authority to increase the number of commissioners and thus the number of ministries, but the Commission has been convinced of the desirability of holding the number to nine. The 1965 treaty on fusion contemplates a brief period of up to three years during which the number of commissioners would be increased to fourteen in order to ease the merger of the twenty-three commissioners of the three communities. Only nine would have to be let go. The 1965 treaty provides, however, for reducing the places to nine again, if not by action of the member governments, then automatically after three years, on the basis of the seniority of the commissioners; and then five more commissioners would be let go.[4]

The commissioners have been men at the height of their careers (in their fifties and sixties), having spent their lives in politics or public administration. The elder members can expect to retire by the time their terms are finished; but the younger still have enough years to accept posts afterwards in their home governments, as one Italian Commissioner did. Death claimed one commissioner, one was elected to the Italian senate, and another left the Commission to become head of the European Coal and Steel Community. The prestige of the Commission is shown by the fact that the head of the secretariat of the Organization of European Economic Cooperation resigned to join it. It is also true, however, that no top political leader has ever served in the Commission, and probably none could be expected to do so until a United States of Europe should materialize and the Commission become the pinnacle of power in Europe.

Does the commissioner talk down to the minister in the Council

⁴ "Traité instituant un conseil unique et une commission unique des communautés européennes." Bruxelles, 8 avril 1965, Arts. 10, 32, 33.

or is it the other way around? The balance has shifted, but generally when those sitting in the Council had a rank no higher than Secretary of State, the commissioners who once held ministerships in their own right could speak before the Council with an air of self-esteem. When, on the other hand, the foreign ministers were sitting in the Council, the tables were turned.

There has been something like a parity of esteem between the most dynamic and powerful two leaders of the Commission, Vice President Mansholt and President Hallstein, and the highest rank-ing members of the Council. President Hallstein had been an author and signer of the Rome Treaty and a protégé of former West German Chancellor Adenauer. Earlier he had been rector of the University of Frankfurt, and he acted habitually as a person of rank. He set up the German foreign office after the Second World War and became famous for the "Hallstein doctrine" against diplo-matic relations with governments that recognized East Germany. Vice President Mansholt had been Dutch minister of agriculture for fourteen years before joining the commission and had intimate knowledge of Dutch politics and residual standing in them; others in the Commission had had ministerial experience. Often com-missioners deal with delegates to the Council who had been their friends and associates in national administration before they "crossed the aisle" into international service.

A majority of the commissioners have been politicians, having had political experience from parliamentary or ministerial service; and, although President Hallstein has never run for public office, he has viewed the work of the Commission as political, not techni-cal. The few businessmen at first in the Commission were later re-placed by politicians, in one case by a French senator of sixteen years parliamentary experience.

It may be axiomatic that the career of a top-level international servant is a history of declining influence. Men cannot *expand* their influence by serving on the Commission. The day has not yet ar-rived when the Common Market is a kingmaker. The commis-sioners while in Brussels have little touch with the public or with party leaders, and their clientele of international civil servants is small. A commissioner has to bring his rank, influence, friendships, and contacts with him to his job if he is to have personal impact outside the household of the Commission. Such influence is slowly perishable at best and can be suddenly reduced by a change of government at home. Men from the smaller Benelux countries are less likely to be forgotten at home.

The choice of men with the confidence of national leaders is indispensable, and, if a commissioner could serve as a scapegoat to overcome an impass in the Council, he would logically be dropped. Hence, elaborate pension arrangements were made for even short-term commissioners.[5] The intensity of the hostility of French Gaullists against Hallstein and Mansholt in 1965 had an inverse effect, however. To have summarily dropped these men was considered offensive by *their* home governments, and they both stayed on. Moreover, controversial commissioners tended to take a self-defeating pride in their waning power in the Council. It made them look more communitarian, and they resisted stepping down.

Under the Rome Treaty, the choice of commissioners was to be made by agreement among the member governments[6]—a provision designed to allow names to be dropped in case one or more governments raised an objection. The choice was actually made on the basis of a detailed gentleman's agreement and on practices and habits the Community fell into. The nine places on the Commission were divided to give each of the three major powers two members and each of the three minor powers one. Originally the presidencies of the three communities were divided among the three great powers, the Coal and Steel Community having been given to Italy, the Atomic Energy Community to France, and the Economic Community to Germany. With the Schuman Plan and Euratom being fused to the Common Market, however, the issue of the presidency of the Commission has had to be reopened. The Council agreed that the presidency would rotate and that the President's two-year reign in the fused Commission could be renewed only once.[7] The arrangement guarantees that an officer over whom controversy arises will leave office after a few years; and standing feuds, such as the De Gaulle-Hallstein feud, have thus been given a time limit.

[5] *Journal officiel,* 5e année, No. 62, 19 juillet 1962, p. 1724.
[6] Communauté économique européenne, *Traité instituant la Communauté économique européenne et documents annexes.* Bruxelles, 1957, Art. 158.
[7] *European Community.* Washington, No. 91, April, 1966, p. 2.

Incidentally, this was the first instance in European constitutional practice in which executive tenure was limited, a practice prevailing already in North and South America where it had been arrived at after a century of study and struggle.

After the presidency, the remaining great powers and one of the minor powers were each allotted a vice presidency; and the most important portfolios were distributed among *them*—agriculture, finance, and interstate commerce. Fusion imposes a four-year tenure limit on vice presidencies, too. The over-all division of portfolios is as follows:

> Germany: administration and antitrust
> France: finance and foreign aid
> Italy: interstate commerce and welfare
> Belgium: foreign relations
> Netherlands: agriculture
> Luxembourg: transport

Italy has replaced its welfare and interstate commerce commissioners more than once, France its foreign aid commissioner and Luxembourg its transport commissioner; but there has been no attempt to reshuffle portfolios among the member states. Although the original division of portfolios was not regarded as permanent, the failure to reshuffle portfolios may have unwanted consequences. France may cling to the foreign aid portfolio, for example, because it is mainly the former French empire that is being aided. Given the problem of poverty in Italy, that country may want to continue to manage social welfare.

There may be some value in continuity in assigning portfolios, but the Community is bound to suffer if its portfolios become "nationalized." Someday the Community may have to face the problem of reassigning portfolios gracefully so as to suit the objective needs of the Community and the capacities of the persons involved. Might there not be some way that a person who distinguishes himself, say, in antitrust affairs can be advanced to the finance portfolio, in the way a cabinet member in a national government can be advanced as his political star is rising? The election of a new commissioner in 1966 occasioned the start of honorific advancement in the Commission. The junior Italian member of the Commission was advanced by the Council to the rank of vice president after the senior Italian member resigned, but the new vice president kept his old portfolio.[8]

Irresponsibility of the Very Young

The Rome Treaty has provided teeth with which the Common Market institutions could scratch and tear one another, but while the institutions were young, gentleness was instinctive. A commissioner may be *suspended* from office by either the Council or the Commission for cause; and, if the cause should be found justified by the Court of Justice, he would be *removed* from office.

The European Parliament may remove the Commissioners *at will*.[9] The Parliament may decide for itself what reasons suffice to overthrow the Commission, and the Commission must then resign in a body. This power has often been discussed in the Parliament, but it has never been used. To have removed the Commission during the Community's youth would have only replaced one half-developed body of officers by another. European parliamentarians asked themselves, however, "At what point will the Commission's power be great enough to make the exercise of the Parliament's sovereign sanction useful?" And some argued that the Commission should be threatened with removal if it did not administer its new responsibilities in the field of agriculture to the Parliament's liking.

There were practical conditions that had to be fulfilled before the removal power could be profitably used. First, the Commission had to have discretionary powers. The treaty gave it some power, but its most important powers were to be conferred on it by the Council as the Council adopted regulations to implement the treaty, a process to be little more than started by the end of the twelve-year transition period. Second, the Commission had to become indispensable to member governments. The governments might not approve of things the Commission did once it fell under parliamentary control; and they would accept the controversial acts of

[8] Communauté économique européenne, Commission, *Huitième rapport général* . . . , juin 1965, p. 449.
[9] *Traité instituant la Communauté économique européenne*, Art. 144.

the Commission only if the Common Market had become so important to them that they could not quit it. By the time of the French boycott of 1965 it would have been *uncomfortable* for France to withdraw from the Common Market, but not *impossible* —and it might not be impossible, perhaps, for decades if ever.

The Rome Treaty placed no check on the Parliament's power to remove the Commission, and if the power comes into use unamended it can produce the *weakest* cabinet (Commission) system in Europe. There is a crying need for at least some provision for the dissolution of Parliament by the Commission if the removal power is used too often. And there might be other safeguards against parliamentary excesses, like those embodied in the constitution of the Fifth French Republic.

Commission or Cabinet?

The Commission was created as a *collegiate* institution whose powers could not be delegated to individual commissioners, and the clumsiness of this arrangement is all too painfully apparent. It means that the Commission has to sit together at least one entire day every week and frequently they meet oftener. They meet Wednesday, the day before the weekly meeting of the permanent representatives where one or more commissioners defend the Commission's proposals; and the commissioners turn out in force to attend the weekly or biweekly meetings of the Council of Ministers and the monthly meetings of the European Parliament.

The atmosphere of the Commission's own meetings is different from that of the Ministers. The meeting room is small and intimate and the only persons present are the commissioners themselves, the chief secretary and the essential clerical personnel. The aides of the commissioners never attend except for brief moments when they are called in to report, after which they leave. The Commission got used to meeting almost alone, because the only appropriate meeting room in the Chateau Val Duchess, where the Commission was initially housed in Brussels, was a room too small to hold the assistants of the commissioners.[10] And at the strong insistence of

[10] Lemaignen, *op. cit.*, p. 30.

President Hallstein a similar room was arranged in the modern building the Commission occupied later. All the original commissioners could understand French, and only one had to express himself in German, which minimized the need for interpreters in meetings of the Commission. German was used in the Commission about a third of the time, and on rare occasions, Dutch. President Hallstein could speak English and all of the Community languages except Dutch. A familylike atmosphere was achieved in the group, and that intimacy was thought to outweigh the value of having staff members present.

The Treaty required the Commission to adopt rules of procedure; but, because of the relative intimacy and informality of its meetings, it postponed doing so for five years. The Treaty specified only that the Commission had to act by a majority vote of five and that it publish its rules, which, since the Commission met in deepest secrecy, amounted to gratuitous information for the public, as will be seen in the next paragraph. The rules that were published finally in 1963 were a mere summary of the Commission's de facto operation.[11]

The collegiate executive was created expressly to prevent a single commissioner (a foreigner to five of the six member nations) from gathering the executive powers of the European Community into his own hands. In Europe, as elsewhere in the world, the average politician believes that an international institution has to have multinational organs, and the collegiate executive looked more trustworthy to outsiders. In practice, the Commission has too many responsibilities to be able to fulfill them collectively. The Commission is faced with a bursting agenda that includes questions all the way from whether airlines should fall under Common Market regulation to whether some usher at headquarters, who has given faithful service, should be allowed to remain at his post after the compulsory retirement age. It has to have a shortcut. Hence, decisions are made in the name of the Commission by individual commissioners. These decisions stand unless, after being circulated to the other commissioners, there is some objection raised; and ordinarily there is no objection. If commissioner A is too strict in

---

[11] *Journal officiel,* 6ᵉ année, No. 17, 31 janvier 1963.

his scrutiny of the decisions of commissioner B, it stands to reason that B will be that much more critical of the decisions of commissioner A. And pride is taken in the number of questions that can be disposed of in this way.[12]

Following a precedent of the Schuman Plan executive, a compromise was struck between individual decisions and collegiate decisions by creating a three-man working group of commissioners for each major policy area. Each commissioner has two others available to him for consultation, and he in return has to help two other groups. By means of these groups practically every policy question can be brought to the point of decision before being placed before the Commission as a whole.

The division of labor in the Commission is not efficient enough by itself. The Commission needs leadership—something to knit it together and give it direction—and that rôle has been played by the President. President Hallstein has been the eldest member of the Commission and the highest paid, and he has had the most illustrious background. He has controlled the "housekeeping" offices in the Common Market, the hiring and firing and spending of money. If he has not had the most persuasive personality, he has been a person one could not long oppose. Most decisions are taken in the Commission without vote, and a President's leverage is always greatest where proceedings are informal. When votes have had to be taken they have usually favored Hallstein's position. If the Rome Treaty had been amended to make Hallstein's authority correspond more closely to that of a president or premier within a national government, the change in fact would not have been a great one.

The Common Market is a dynamic institution, moving very rapidly and knowing where it is going; and it was ready for a leader with Hallstein's temerity. Hallstein has accelerated the execution of the treaty, moved into uncertain policy areas without hesitation, addressed statesmen and audiences on all continents as the agent and spokesman for Europe, and proclaimed the United States of Europe in identifying within the existing Community the embryo of the political institution that could make that dream a

[12] Cf. Emile Noël, Speech to Conservative Political Center, Oxford, England, July 7, 1962 [mimeographed].

reality. The Commission's exuberance born of rapid success left it psychologically unprepared for the shock when France vetoed British membership in January, 1963, and seemed to end the Community's winning streak; but there was no doubt that optimistic leadership during the first half decade was a factor in the good fortune of the Community.

Leadership in the Commission has two important limitations. First, the lower-ranking members are proud to be members and jealous of the prerogatives of their offices. They are quick to assert the essential legal equality among all commissioners, whether they can in fact act independently of the President or not. Thus, de facto leadership has to be cultivated constantly or lost.

Second, truly collegiate action is the only way to resolve a clash of national interests within the Commission. In theory the Commission represents the interests of the Community as a whole as opposed to the Council of Ministers, which represents nations; but there is a fallacy in this theory in that it fails to take account of the communitarian leanings of the Council and ignores the national biases of the commissioners. Portfolios had to be distributed among commissioners in such a way as to leave the most sensitive problems, i.e., agriculture, tariff-disarmament, and foreign relations, in the "neutral" hands of the Netherlands, Italy, and Belgium, respectively. France and Germany were so likely to collide over these issues that their nationals were not trusted to be impartial.

Nationalities are mixed in the administrative heirarchy of the Commission, and that does place French and German officials in conflict, however. The French Commissioner Robert Lemaignen, in charge of associated former colonies, wrote of just such a collision with his German executive officer. Lemaignen wanted Common Market privileges for the former French colonies, while the director of his staff echoed the desire of Germany to treat all African nations equally regardless of their former relation to France. And so Lemaignen had the director replaced.[13] Lemaignen's implied justification of his action was that the Community should share *France's* policy toward her former colonies. Other commissioners expected the Community to espouse the positions of their respective governments, and each was convinced that his way was the best way for

[13] Lemaignen, *op. cit.*, pp. 146-147.

Europe to follow, as when Hallstein shared the isolated position of the German government on Community agricultural policy only to be outvoted by his colleagues and to see his leadership momentarily lapse.

Each commissioner is nominated to the Commission by some political leader at home to whom he then owes a debt of gratitude and for whom he may have a lot of respect. A commissioner has to maintain his contacts and influence in his own government if he is to help move proposals toward adoption in the Council of Ministers; and, unless he is old enough to expect to retire after his service with the Commission, he has to rely on his political friends at home to give him a good job when he returns home. Commissioner Petrilli resigned from the Commission, for example, to head up the state business enterprises of the Italian government. It is difficult to draw a line between the *consultation* with commissioners by national officials and the *instruction* of commissioners, and commissioners protest the purely international motivation for their actions so often they arouse suspicion. There is no reason to think that this pattern could be any different. Every politician in any form of government must originate in some region and have special sensitivity to the interests of that region. The problem for the European Community is not so much that of finding executive personnel who are devoid of regional associations as it is one of adjusting to the idea that nationals of *one* country can be trusted to handle the affairs of *all* the member countries.

Days in Council

Like a performing artist whose rehearsals, though vital, are incidental to performances, the Commission's machinations within its own household are no more than incidental to its performances before the Council of Ministers. It is those performances that are its work, because the progress of the Common Market has been measured by the Commission's success in getting the Council to approve its proposals. All the rest is preparatory.

When meeting with the Council, the Commission behaves with respect, but with dignity and with a consciousness of its prerogatives.

The Treaty is silent on practical arrangements between Commission and Council, but the Commission has worked hard to develop as close and easy a relationship with the Council as possible. All the commissioners attend when they are able, and at least the President and those commissioners who have specialized in the subject of each agenda are present. Commissioners' chief aides sit for them when they have to be absent. The President normally speaks for the group, and, since the statements of the Commission are apt to be explanations of new proposals, he speaks characteristically with the voice of a teacher, a tonality President Hallstein has already exercised in the classroom. Compromises there have had to be, but they have been made in such a way as to protect the Commission's self-respect; and at times the Commission has scolded the Council for its slowness in bringing matters to decision. The influence of the Commission in the Council is largely due to the political vocation of the Commissioners themselves, which affects the manner in which proposals are framed, the way support and opposition are predicted, and the way meetings are addressed and corridor diplomacy conducted. The fact that the Council depends on the Commission for a great deal of research also gives special credence to the views of the commissioners who have overseen the research.

The Council and the Commission have often differed on methods to implement the Rome Treaty, and so the interplay between the Council and the Commission has been the tensest arena of politics in the Community. By no means is the Commission merely the administrative handmaiden of the Council, since there are two forms of leverage the Commission can use against the Council. First, the Commission's power of initiative gives it the jump on the Council in that it can advance its own interpretation of the Treaty and then, with the Council obligated to implement the Treaty, call on the Council to adopt *that* interpretation. The Council's ability to resist this leverage, however, is stronger than the Commission's power to exert it. The Commission, knowing that there is no way to implement the Treaty other than through the Council, has little choice but to accept changes the Council wishes to make in its proposals. The Commission can afford to be coldly steadfast in its position if the Council is divided over an issue, because it stands a chance of becoming the rallying point for a majority in the Council. But, when several delegates side against the Commission, the commissioners can gain little by further resistance, and a timely compromise can win Council approval. On one occasion when the Council was adopting a regulation on the free movement of workers, the Commission was asked to remove the provision that migrant workers be eligible to hold offices in labor unions, but the Commission refused. It was not until sometime later in the same meeting that the Commission realized it would get nowhere by resisting and requested a recess to prepare an amendment of its own, which, when further debated and amended, was suitable for adoption at the next Council meeting a month later.

Second, the Treaty provides a special voting formula that makes it difficult for the Council to amend the Commission's proposals. The Council can adopt many proposals of the Commission by a qualified majority vote, but it has to adopt *unanimously* any amended proposals *opposed* by the Commission. In other words, the Commission needs only one ally in the Council to prevent the amendment of a proposal. But there is little profit in clinging to the original terms of a proposal if it cannot get sufficient support for adoption—it is better to accept the amendments as part of the original proposal. When the Commission was defending its first proposal regarding equalization of freight rates, it willingly accepted amendments proposed by the members of the Council and, in fact, suggested possible amendments in order to spur agreement. Of what value were the Commission's views compared with achieving agreement among conflicting positions in the Council? Why would the Commission wish to force use of the unanimous voting formula and increase the difficulty of adopting its proposal? Sometimes the Commission *did* invoke the unanimity rule on amendments when it was unusually certain of the strength or rectitude of its position, as in the case of its draft budgets and financial proposals, where it had the Council over a barrel.[14] The Council had to accept the Commission's draft, change it by unanimous amendments, or close the shop. The Commission had little to lose by rigidity here.

There has always been a realm of policy making in which co-

---

[14] P.-H. J. M. Houben, *Les Conseils de Ministres des Communautés Européennes.* Leyden: A. W. Sythoff, 1964, p. 120.

operation was the key, where the use of leverage was out of the question, and where the Commission acted smoothly as a preparatory body whose work the Council readily approved. Members of the Council will even agree informally to take action recommended by the Commision as an adjunct to Community regulations, though not required by them, as was true of an understanding in the Council to limit rebates in the poultry trade.[15] The main purpose of the French boycott of 1965 to 1966 was to force the Community to restrict its policy making to this area of common agreement, but it was because the Commission and the other members of the Council wished to press beyond the dead center of complete concensus that the French were resisted. It was in the Commission's use of constitutional leverage that the Common Market tested and strengthened its integrity. The Commission was doing its best in the Council, in other words, when it was doing its worst.

[15] Question écrite No. 109, *Journal officiel,* 8ᵉ année, No. 45, 19 mars 1965 p. 678.

The Administration

IV

From the beginning, the civil service of the Common Market was in upheaval. The transition period during which new offices had to be created incessantly was to last twelve years. If new member governments were admitted, they would demand a share of the posts. And with staff offices scattered all over Brussels, in Luxembourg, and in Strasbourg, traveling has been an everyday punishment for many officers. Moreover, the Community has had to face the possibility that it might have to *move*.

A House Is Not a Home

Europe has had no capital, only pretenders. There is no European statesman who can be precise in explaining what the implications of the selection of one capital or another would be, so much mythology is attached to the idea of a European capital. The European Community had to give up hope of an early selection of a permanent headquarters, because the aspirations of member governments were so strong. "Why not Rome," asked the Italians, "which is the traditional imperial capital and the city where the Community treaties were signed?" "Why not a 'federal district,'" asked the French, "at Chantilly just outside Paris (famous for lace, a race track, and the monument to the German surrender to the French in the forest nearby)?" "Community institutions are already situated on our territory," said France, Belgium, and Luxembourg, "why not centralize them all there?" What was at stake was prestige, and the Commission did not deceive itself that the long residence in Brussels would necessarily make that city the European capital. The transfer of much larger capitals was known to have occurred: Rio to Brazilia, Karachi to Islamabad, and Tel Aviv to Jerusalem.

The importance of establishing a permanent headquarters of the Community has grown every year, because the provisional character of the existing headquarters is a dead weight on the efficiency of the organization. It has been difficult to pry loose the institutions of the Community from Luxembourg and Strasbourg. "Why should those offices be let go," said the fathers of these municipalities, "until it is certain where they are going ultimately?" These cities are each bidding to become the capital of Europe too and do not wish to erase their names from the everyday language of the Community by giving up their link with it. Unlike the United Nations, which owns its own real estate, the Community has had to lease its real estate; and compromises have had to be made every step of the way. Although Brussels considers itself a major contender to be the capital of Europe and has spent money on urban improvements keyed to this prospect, including the building of new structures to house the Community, it must always guard itself against the possiblity that some day the organization may decide to go elsewhere. From the standpoint of the Community it is more important that a decision on a permanent capital be made soon than that it be made in favor of Brussels.

Two types of factors bear on the choice of a capital—political factors and geographic.[1] Two members of the Community did not bid for the capital, Germany and the Netherlands. The inability of Germany to establish itself as the capital of Europe after a passage of arms in the 1940's virtually eliminated the possibility that it would be made a European capital by peaceful means during the 1960's. And the Dutch language was not broadly enough known in the Community to make Holland a feasible home. Other governments that *are* bidding for the capital have marked weaknesses. The eccentric geographical position of Italy in relation to the

---

[1] For a scientific survey of geographic factors bearing on the choice of a European capital see Saul B. Cohen, *Geography and Politics in a World Divided.* New York: Random House, 1963, pp. 166-172.

other members of the Community militates against its choice for a capital. The experience of the Coal and Steel Community in Luxembourg has downgraded that country as a possibility in much the same way that the experience of the League of Nations in Geneva ruled out that city as a possible seat for the United Nations. Geneva and Luxembourg are lovely cities, but neither is on an aorta of communication in Europe, which is vital to the business and social life of the people working in the institutions.

The most serious contenders remain, then, France and Belgium. The French case is strong. Already the centrality of Strasbourg (France) has caused it to be made the headquarters of the Council of Europe; and, too, the precise geographic center of the Community falls somewhere in France. But a provincial city like Strasbourg is bound to suffer from the same disabilities as Luxembourg or Geneva. It is Paris or one of its modern satellite cities that is the real rival of Brussels, and some geographic factors are in its favor. It is so close to Brussels that it shares the centrality of that city while being slightly closer to Italy. Paris, too, has much the same attraction in Europe as New York has in America in being such an important business and cultural center. Other European institutions such as the North Atlantic Treaty Organization and the Organization for Economic Cooperation and Development have been attracted to Paris.[2] Moreover, the advanced state of crowding and dilapidation in parts of Paris make some plan for urban renewal almost inevitable. And, if such renewal were keyed to the building of a new capital for Europe, this jewel could have a very carefully constructed setting.

On the other hand, the way the French government pursued its case lessened the possibility of an early choice of Paris or of any other permanent headquarters. The nationalistic tenor of French participation in the Community during the Gaullist era gave special sharpness to the reasons for keeping the capital out of France. France has a natural position of importance in European politics, but when France becomes the chief proponent of its own importance, as in the French (Fouchet) proposal for a European political community, which designated Paris as the Community's

---

[2] Paris is also the host city of more international organizations and associations than any other city in the world.

permanent home,[3] the whole picture changes. France cannot insist upon being the leader of Europe, because she has no decisive leverage. Her mantle of leadership is worn most effectively when it is worn loosely. Although the Germans may have felt incapable of asserting a claim to the capital themselves, they are almost certain to act unfavorably to any idea that France has a right to the capital.

Brussels has been a useful compromise. Its being fixed upon as the temporary capital was no accident, just as the choosing of New York as the temporary (now permanent) headquarters of the United Nations was no accident. Although the European Commission has maintained a polite silence on its preference for a capital, the European Parliament forthrightly recommended that a European "federal district" be established in Brussels, and the Brussels city fathers offered to convert a little-used military drill field in the Southeast corner of the city to that purpose. The provisional location of the Commission has been a better place for a European capital, however. The original offices occupied real estate near the eye of the newer part of Brussels, the Cinquantenaire Park, with its triumphal arch, royal museums, monuments, gardens, and wide converging avenues—all an easy quarter of an hour by super highway from the new Brussels airport.

The Brussels World's Fair of 1958 made Brussels an especially accommodating host to the Community, because the fair occasioned massive urban development. Internal superhighways were built; and the charmingly decrepit Mont des Arts district was replaced by a modern complex of buildings, which the Community promptly leased for its Council of Ministers. Equally important, there was a frenzy of private real estate speculation, and modern apartment houses rose around the edges of the city. These provided room for the thousands of secretariat members that had to be assembled almost overnight, and no other European capital could have accommodated the influx. Brussels is almost equidistant from not only Paris, Luxembourg, Bonn and the Hague, but also London, the greatest potential addition to the Community. Dutch and French, the languages of four Community countries, are native to

[3] Article 9 of the original plan, found in European Parliament, Political Committee, *Towards Political Union,* January, 1964, p. 13.

Brussels, and English is widely spoken there. Although Brussels cannot match the urban resources of such cities as Rome, Berlin, or Paris, it is cosmopolitian in its own right and does not suffer the provincial limitations of Luxembourg or Strasbourg. When the headquarters of the North Atlantic Treaty Organization had to leave the Paris area after the withdrawal of French forces from NATO command in 1966, Brussels proved to be NATO's logical new home.

Curing a Split Personality

The lack of a permanent capital was only one of the early headaches of the Community. Another was the administrative separation among the three communities. The Community has had only one court, one parliament, and one secretariat for its Councils of Ministers; and a few administrative functions were unified. But the main body of the civil service was split in three. Any decision making that entailed cooperation among the three administrations was difficult—transportation policy, for instance, or energy policy.

There was no question of the lesser administrations simply being swept up in enthusiasm for the Common Market. The Coal and Steel Community had been in existence for six years before the Common Market started. Its executive body was sensitive about the possibility that certain rule-making powers it possessed might be nullified by too close an association with the Common Market executive, which had less rule-making power at first. Also the Coal and Steel Community was proud of its experience and felt justified in remaining aloof from the Common Market's enthusiasms until that body had passed its international childhood. Officials in Luxembourg could only nod knowingly as the Brussels Commission received spankings from the French government, beginning with the rebuff of the Commission's proposal to have diplomatic representation in Washington and London and reaching a climax in the boycott that blocked the Commission's request for independent sources of revenue.

Also, two governments, France and Luxembourg, stood in the way of fusing the three communities. The Gaullist government resisted the development of supranational administration in the Community; and, if the administration could be kept split, its development could be slowed. To the good fortune of the Community, however, one ground on which the French vetoed British membership in 1963 was that British worldwide connections would counteract Community integrity. And one of the first gestures of the French to make good this claim of integrity was to reverse their stand against fusing the communities. Still Luxembourg's opposition sufficed to block a change, because the Treaty required unanimity in the Council of Ministers. What Luxembourg stood to lose were the income and prestige that the Coal and Steel Community had brought it. And of these two, for wealthy Luxembourg the matter of prestige was decisive. Moreover, popularly elected officials in Luxembourg had pledged to keep the body and could not let it go without betraying their constituents.

After the French had come around, the pressure then exerted on Luxembourg was partially successful. Luxembourg agreed to let most of the Community people go to Brussels but insisted on remaining the headquarters for the European Court, the secretariat of the European Parliament, and the financial offices of the Community.[4] On April 8, 1965, the Fusion Treaty was signed, but actual implementation of the move was delayed by the French boycott of 1965.

The Fusion Treaty was short. The fused Commission was authorized to "rationalize" the civil service, meaning to unite it in Brussels. Problems of amalgamating the special powers of the Coal and Steel Community with the fused Community were skirted by retaining the language of earlier treaties, which left the coal-and-steel powers intact, though in new hands. On a few points adjustments had to be made, and in such cases the coal-and-steel regime was modified to harmonize with the Brussels regime. Formerly, voting in coal-and-steel councils had been weighted according to *variables,* such as coal and steel production; but the new treaty *fixed* the number of votes for each nation in line with voting

[4] Decision des représentants des Gouvernements des Etats membres, relative à l'installation provisoire de certaines Institutions et de certains services des Communautés." Bruxelles, 8 avril 1965.

weights laid down in the Rome Treaty.[5] The tax on coal and steel production levied by the Luxembourg office was prevented from becoming a general revenue source for the fused Community by putting a ceiling on the amount of money that could be so collected.[6]

The process of ratifying the treaty was long. Since the French were backing the treaty and ratified it right away, the French boycott against the other members in 1965 slowed down ratification elsewhere. The Dutch were tempted to pigeonhole the treaty until the French promised not to try to strip the Community of its supranational powers when its three founding treaties were eventually rewritten into a single document. The Belgians wanted to have a preliminary understanding as to just who would serve as officers and members of the fused Commission of fourteen before depositing ratification; and so as of the present writing, no ratifications have been deposited.[7]

The fusion of the three communities promises to heal only part of Europe's split personality. There are still nearly three dozen autonomous international organizations in Europe; and, although there is variation in their membership, most of them have about fifteen members, not six.[8] Organizations such as the Council of Europe or the Conference of European Ministers of Transport serve a wider Europe and could gain nothing from amalgamation with the Community of the Six. The system for the protection of human rights that was set up by the Council of Europe is just as effective as any measure of the Community—possibly more so because of the large number of adherents. And the Conference of the Ministers of Transport is so useful a format for cooperation that it impinges on the freedom of the Community to act in transport matters. The railroad chiefs of Europe prefer to deal with their problems in the round with all affected administrations participating. Decisions of the Six, though important, can deal with only

[5] "Traité instituant un conseil unique et une commission unique des communautées européennes." Bruxelles, 8 avril 1965, Art. 8.

[6] *Ibid.*, Art. 20, Para. 2.

[7] Communauté économique européenne, Commission, *Neuvième rapport général* . . . , juin 1966, p. 390.

[8] Average based on listings in Union of International Associations, *Yearbook of International Organization,* 10th ed. Brussels, 1964.

a part of European railroading. The admission of the members of the European Free Trade Association to the Common Market would make the membership of the Community approximately the same as most European organizations and would be a long step toward further fusion of international institutions in Europe. But to know the treatment for European organizational schizophrenia does not ease the long task of therapy. In the meantime the Common Market has to try to protect its interests. When European organizational steps threaten to skirt the Community, they have to be fought against lest some new field be preempted from the Community. Beginning in the fall of 1966, the Common Market Commission tried to block a new organization to regulate the construction and demolition of Rhine boats that was being created within the framework of the widely international Rhine Commission instead of in the framework of the Common Market; but the outcome of the attempt cannot be predicted.

The Idea Machine

The Common Market Commission's profession is to prepare a continual flow of proposals, and that work necessitates thousands of civil servants. It assembled about a thousand workers the first year (1958) by raiding the national civil services, from which some of the best talent of Europe was secured on loan. Afterwards, the staff of the Commission increased on the average of 200 per year so that by 1966 it reached 3,320. The three communities called a hiring holiday for the year 1966 so as to help uncomplicate their anticipated fusion, but the act of fusion itself would give the appearance of sudden expansion to all persons involved. To the fast-growing thousands of Common Market administrators were to be added the relatively static numbers of administrators of the Coal and Steel Community (900) and the equally static numbers (760) of Euratom administrators, plus the operational personnel (2,500) of Euratom engaged in research or the support of research. The number of Euratom operatives jumps by hundreds whenever new laboratories or research installations are opened. If one includes, finally, the 580 administrative employees of the services

that were already shared among the communities,[9] the household
of the fused executive promised to begin with a complement of
8,060. The total personnel of the three communities in 1966, including the separate secretariats of the Court, the Council, the
Parliament, and the European Investment Bank was 9,460—nine
thousand in nine years since the Rome Treaty.

Before the fusion became imminent, the employees of the Coal
and Steel Community looked with envy at the offices in Brussels and
sought jobs there, and the prospect of being absorbed by the Common Market promised to bring the peripheral agencies into the
main arena of European politics. Still, Schuman Plan employees
were fearful that, in the merging of budgets and the administrative
reshuffling that would follow fusion, newcomers would lose out to
the civil servants already ensconced in Brussels.

The cost of administration and operations is borne by the member
states according to a combination of formulas, and the Benelux
countries are spared some of the financial obligations faced by the
three big nations. For example, France, Germany, and Italy each
pay 28 per cent of the administrative budget of the Common Market; Belgium and the Netherlands, 7.9 per cent each; and Luxembourg, 0.2 per cent.[10] The Rome Treaty allowed the Common
Market to propose alternative revenue sources to member governments and suggested that the Community's tariff could provide
such money, but it did not limit the methods the Community
might choose for self-support.[11] In 1965, when the Commission
proposed that the Community be given the direct revenue from
the common tariff, it was sternly rebuked by the French government on the grounds that the Community was not yet democratic
enough to have revenue of its own. The French, moreover, were in
no mood to allow further democratization of Community institutions.

The Community cost $600 million during 1966, of which only
$84 million was spent by the Euratom and Schuman Plan offices
of the Community. The Common Market expenditures were mainly

---

[9] The legal, statistical, and information services.
[10] Communauté économique européenne, *Traité instituant la Communauté
économique européenne et documents annexes*. Bruxelles, 1957, Art. 200.
[11] *Ibid.*, Art. 201.

for subsidies, such as the Social Fund ($20 million) aimed at re-
lieving economic distress caused by the creation of the Common
Market, the Agricultural Fund ($300 million) for financing the
Community's farm price control system, and the European Development Fund ($130 million) for aiding the African states associated
with the Community. Such operations promised to change the fi-
nances of the Community out of all recognition within a few years.
The Agricultural Fund alone was expected to cost another half
billion dollars per year by 1970, and the increasing emphasis being
placed on nuclear power production presaged a mammoth increase
in Euratom operations.

Approximately $300 million more passed through Community
hands in 1966, but it could not be classed with the costs of the
Community because it was in the form of loans that had to be
paid back. About half the amount was new loans by the European
Investment Bank (EIB), an "independent" Common Market agency,
directed by the finance ministers of the Six, that invests in chiefly
industrial, transport, and power enterprises to help boost development opportunities in depressed regions of the Community. More
than half of its investment was in Southern Italy, although the
Southwestern half of France and the associate members Greece and
Turkey were important recipients, too. Investments by the EIB are
only a small fraction of total European investment in any given
year, but it is a useful mechanism. Like the World Bank it had
its capital subscribed by the member governments ($1 billion), who
paid in only a quarter of their subscriptions, and that was lent out.
The remaining capital stands as a guarantee to private lenders who
lend the Bank money on the private capital market. In essence
the EIB is a guarantor, promoter, and middle man for private investment in Community interests. The remaining half of the 1966
loan money was lent by the Schuman Plan to coal and steel firms.
Again it was only a small fraction of total investment in the industry in that year, and the role of the European Coal and Steel
Community (ECSC) has been the same as that of the EIB—it
borrows money to lend it for Community purposes.

The Coal and Steel Community was authorized to levy a tax
on coal and steel production, which not only covered its expenses
from 1952 onward but was an embarrassment of riches, necessitating

repeated *reductions* in the annual tax rates. The Fusion Treaty, however, put a ceiling of $18 million on receipts from the tax (approximately the actual level of receipts for 1962 to 1963) so as to guard coal and steel producers against being exploited for activities not beneficial to them; and that ceiling relegated the coal and steel tax to a minor role in the future financing of the combined communities. The Common Market farm regulations of 1962 provided for the receipt by the Community of the levies on agricultural trade beginning in 1970,[12] but the revenue from that source was expected to cover only half the anticipated cost of the price control system in 1970. The backbone of Community finances, in other words, would remain the contributions of member governments until such time as other independent sources of revenue were decided upon.

Garnering contributions from governments is never easy, and the Council of Ministers holds an iron grip on the purse strings. Other Community institutions can propose or advise, but the Council always decides, and that is a power for which the European Parliament has had the greatest envy. When the Common Market started out, its founding governments had not appropriated any money to it at all. It had to live on loans from the Schuman Plan organization. New projects later on, such as the loan promised to Greece under the terms of Greek association with the Community, saw a lag in governmental contributions, too. The Commission was instructed by the Council to go ahead and negotiate the Greek loan, and yet each government was saying it would not contribute to the loan unless the others did. It then took eighteen months of haggling before money was forthcoming.[13]

The employees of the Common Market are nonpolitical with some important exceptions. There is a small staff or "cabinet" of compatriots surrounding each commissioner, who work closely with him; and at the insistence of President Hallstein the cabinets have been kept small (two or three persons) so as to avoid nationalizing the departments. The staff does the commissioner's leg work for

[12] Communauté économique européenne, le Conseil, Réglement No. 25 relatif au financement de la politique agricole commune, *Journal officiel*, 5ᵉ année, No. 30, 20 avril 1962.

[13] Robert Lemaignen, *L'Europe au Berceau*. Paris: Plom, 1964, pp. 206-207.

him in sounding out the positions of national administrations and the other commissioners, and they represent him at Community meetings he is unable to attend. Politics is their everyday concern.

The immediate subordinates of the commissioners, the general directors, usually have had administrative, rather than political backgrounds, and frequently they have been associated with some aspect of international administration or with the movement for European integration. Usually they are about a decade younger than the commissioners; and, unless they intend to finish out their careers in the Common Market directorships (there has been little chance of their being made commissioners) they have to keep one eye on their home governments, which are their most likely alternative employers. The French government has considered their nationals among the upper Eurocrats as being on leave from their bureaus at home and has wanted them back after five years, but that idea has not been followed by the other governments.[14] The Commission assures a permanent, close link between national and international administration by soliciting approval from each government for its nationals being appointed to professional posts in Brussels;[15] and all the Eurocrats at the top policy-making level were nominated by governments at the very start of the Common Market.[16]

The thousands of nonpolitical personnel lower down the hierarchy include all Community nationalities. They hold permanent tenure, are free from instruction by governments, and are exempt from any action by the Belgian host government that might affect their work. No debt of gratitude is owed by individual civil servants to sponsors in the home governments because the international posts are filled by open competition and examinations. It was only at the beginning that it was necessary to ask national departments to loan large numbers of civil servants to Brussels.

One reason Eurocrats have to watch for openings in their home administrations is that the Common Market is victim to the same pressures for geographical distribution of staff that make life so difficult for the United Nations Secretariat. That is to say, in order

[14] Leon Lindberg, *The Political Dynamics of European Economic Integration.* Stanford, Calif.: Stanford University Press, 1963, p. 85.
[15] *Ibid.,* p. 73.
[16] *Ibid.,* p. 55.

to avoid the nationalization of any particular Common Market department the nationalities of the staff are required to *alternate* in the hierarchy. Thus a commissioner would have a general director of a nationality different from his; the general director's assistant would be of a different nationality still, and so on down the line. Promotions of any kind are difficult. For example, if A is Belgian and his subordinate B is French and in turn B's subordinate C is Belgian, C cannot be promoted in the same hierarchy because, if he were, there would be two Belgians next to one another in the ranks. The intricacies of subject matter might prevent him from being promoted into another department, and so he might have little alternative to going back to his home government should some opportunity knock.

The artificialities and uncertainties of such a regime have been the occasion for anomalies such as when in 1963 the position of General Director for Social Affairs remained without an occupant for half a year while a candidate of the appropriate nationality was being found. The system of alternating nationalities in the ranks is not totally rigid, but Common Market morale would improve if the system did not exist at all. No tradition would be violated in scrapping the system, because the Coal and Steel Community, from which the Common Market borrowed most of its personnel rules, never had such a system. Officially, the alternation system is hailed as a safeguard for the communitarian character of the staff, but it might equally be viewed as a sign of mistrust of the communitarian instincts of the staff members.

Moreover, alternation of nationalities failed to prevent nationalization of departments. What counts is the nationality of the man on top. The expression of views characteristic of other nationalities in the staff can be treated as insubordination. Since the alternation principle prevents commissioners from having their own protégés as general directors, the general directors offices are filled by the trading of protégés among the Commissioners.[17] Commissioner Lemaignen, who was the Frenchman in charge of overseas territories for the Community, took on a German general director but asked the German government for another when the first committed the error of expressing in public an attitude toward overseas territories

[17] Cf. Lemaignen, *op. cit.,* p. 68.

that was different from Lemaignen's.[18] In other words, the alternation principle was not to be allowed to produce a contest over policy. Its function has simply been to make the department *look* international. This is what is best called the "zoo" theory of international staffing, collecting many species, all safely in cages.

There were bound to be special pressures on the Commission in the personnel field. What with the European governments contributing more to the Common Market administration than they had to any other international organization in the past, assurances were demanded that there would be a sharing of posts among the nationalities; and agreement was reached upon a quota system under which each of the big three members and the Benelux members together would have one-quarter of the administrative posts. Within the Benelux group the ratio was 2:2:1 for Belgium, the Netherlands, and Luxembourg. But these ratios could have been observed without the alternating principle.

In order to compensate for the disruptions and arbitrary and dead-end disadvantages of international administration, the pay scales were set high.[19] To put it another way, the Community had to buy its way into the talent market at a premium. The Schuman Plan bought in at too high a rate, or so it seemed to the Council of Ministers when they set the pay and pension standards of the Common Market at a lower rate. The personnel did not see eye to eye with the Council, however. They organized and were able to force a pay raise on the Community that made Common Market personnel costs jump $5 million between 1965 and 1966, but the 1966 pay increase was still only six per cent. The staff was demanding *fourteen* per cent, and so on March 22, 1966, they staged a twenty-four hour walkout in Brussels and Luxembourg to demonstrate their solidarity. It was reported to be ninety-seven per cent effective, although some participation was squelched by President Hallstein who *ordered* interpreters to keep serving the official

[18] *Ibid.,* pp. 146-147.

[19] The Council of Ministers went a long way toward normalizing life in the secretariat when it adopted personnel regulations effective January 1, 1962. These were based on the Regulations of the Coal and Steel Community, and they were due to be superseded by a common body of regulations for the fused Community.

decision-making bodies.[20] The upshot of the strike was discussion of a compromise on a ten per cent raise.

Asking the interpreters to report for work entailed for the Common Market an unusually large number of persons, because the institution had become the largest employer of interpreters in the world, having surpassed the United Nations in that respect in 1966. Every written word has to be published in four languages (Dutch, French, German, and Italian) and sometimes five or six (English and Spanish), and working committees or lawmaking organs can be addressed in any of the Community languages. French serves as a kind of common denominator in public rooms, in the corridors, among strangers, and among persons who do not know one another's languages. But the marshaling of the army of interpreters around Commission headquarters and the occasional crises in their recruitment and training create a distinction between the Common Market's administration and the administration of national governments more conspicuously than any other single thing.[21]

The Eurocrats provide Brussels with a new high-salaried group, who live in better parts of town, thus bringing new commerce to the city but possibly driving up real estate prices. They are insulated from outside interference by a protocol on privileges and immunities. The protocol, newly revised in the Fusion Treaty, is a brief document merely exempting officials from responsibility for their official acts and from liability to taxation or import duties. It follows the modern trend away from traditional diplomatic immunities, a trend much advanced by European organizations in trying to appear as much as possible like ordinary administrative offices and not like international enclaves. The average staff member has little reason to know or invoke his privileges and immunities except when he first arrives in Belgium, at which time he can enter with his household goods and car duty free. He is scarcely conscious of being exempt from national income taxes, because the Common Market levies an income tax on its employees to free staff members of the embarrassment of being tax free in the midst of Belgian

[20] *New York Times,* March 23, 1966.
[21] Based on the intimate account by Alistair Reed, "Lost in Translation," *The New Yorker,* XXXIX, No. 29, 1963, pp. 43-74.

nationals who pay income taxes. The only individuals who have felt slighted by the privileges and immunities are the Belgian Eurocrats who had no opportunity to bring in their cars duty free, since they were already in Belgium when hired.

Staff members are allowed to display a license plate painted blue at one end and bearing the abbreviation EUR; and the special plate may have been a good public relations idea in that it is constantly advertising the Common Market to the Belgian and neighboring publics. The United Nations, by contrast, abandoned its early attempt to use its own license plates when there developed strong resentment in New York against this apparent device for legitimizing parking abuses. The European citizen is by nature less aggressively egalitarian than the New Yorker and is used to such symbols of privilege as the CD license plates that mark cars of the *corps diplomatique*. Still it may have been a mistake for the Common Market to associate itself with the CD plates, which have no apparent role other than to allow foreign-service personnel to make a habit of infringing traffic regulations.

In a less conspicuous way, the Community altered the civic life of Brussels and five other cities that host Community offices by instituting *European* schools, which enrolled over six thousand in 1966. The initiative was taken by the Coal and Steel Community in Luxembourg where it built a modern school building in the shape of an E and with a huge E emblazoned over its entrance. It was the language problem, the bane of international organizations, that necessitated the schools, because the children of Eurocrats are often too young to know foreign languages. Headship of the schools was vested in the Registrar of the Community Court, which kept them out of politics as much as possible, but there has been trouble anyway. The European school at Mol, Belgium, violated the Belgian legislation that made all schools in the country unilingual, because the European schools were multilingual and required more than one language in their curriculum as befitted a *European* education. Belgian politics was extremely sensitive on the point because of the tense opposition between Wallonian- and Flemish-speaking Belgians who would rather riot than learn one another's languages. But ultimately the Community triumphed. It threatened to close the European schools in Belgium (a black eye for Belgium) and in all the other Community countries (which wanted the schools enough to put pressure on the Belgian government).

To prevent warping the children by exposing them to civil servants' children only, an equal number of local students are accepted at the schools, and competition for admission among the latter group is keen. The job of an international school is a hard one, because the Eurocrats' children often feel "away from home" and tend to form cliques with children who speak their own language, but the rewards from implementing an advanced European curriculum are great for all parties concerned.

When Is Administration Administration?

The idea machine of the Common Market required thousands of employees, because the Eurocrats had to study methods for harmonizing national policies on almost every conceivable subject, social security systems, marketing for every category of produce, rights and restrictions of business, banking and currency standards, foreign aid, etc. The list of subjects of legislation awaiting harmonization seemed inexhaustible, and the Eurocrats could do no more than make an efficient start, adding new personnel and opening up new subjects as fast as humanly possible. Harmonizing the legislation of six nations is not a product that can be ground out on a piece-rate basis by an army of industrious civil servants. Contentious issues are raised every step of the way, and these have to be tackled by specialized committees. The administration in Brussels is laced with committees of its own, and on most days at least a dozen such groups can be found locked in discussion. The points of view of outsiders are consulted too. The Committees of the European Parliament meet with Commission personnel in Brussels every month for exchanges of views on draft proposals of the Commission. And consultations with other outsiders are routinized in such standing committees as the Monetary Committee, the Business Cycles Committee, the Budget Committee, the Medium Term Planning Committee, the European Development Fund Committee. It became habitual for the Council of Ministers to set up a committee of its own members or a committee of experts from the national governments to take part in each new area of policy-making consultations. The exchanges of views are not confined to Brussels, and frequently the members of the Commission and their aides make tours of member capitals to speak with responsible officials.

The snarl of policy-making committees consists of many historical threads, each leading in its own way toward solution of some Community problem. There are no two alike, but tracing the policies initiated in the agricultural field can illustrate the kinds of help the Eurocrats give to the Community's lawmaking. The Commission convened an agricultural conference at Stresa in 1958. It then devoted a year to the study of the entire European agricultural system and came up with a preliminary proposal. The next year was spent in consultations with committees of the Parliament and the Council, which led in 1960 to the presentation by the Commission of its final recommendation—a book of 450 pages including statistical material that was the product of millions of man-hours of preparatory work. The Council accepted the scheme in principle and requested the Commission to prepare draft regulations on farm produce—one for each category, e.g., grain, rice, beef, poultry, etc. Still more committees for consultation were set up; and in the course of the following year, drafts were prepared that defined regulatory principles and established the timetable by which those standards were to be met. The regulations were modified and adopted by the Council on January 14, 1962, after a two hundred hour marathon meeting.

Much remained to be done, because the principles and timetables would not implement themselves. It was necessary to organize the immense market-reporting network that would be permanently necessary in operating the new regime and, on the basis of that reporting, prepare specific price schedules and a system of financing for subsidized crops. The Eurocrats also had to offer the Council fateful proposals of Community-wide prices for each category of produce when required by the timetables.

The Eurocrats had only two years to accustom themselves to the oversight of the multifaceted system when the time came to set a common price for grain, politically the most volatile issue the Common Market had faced. Eurocrats had studied the situation Community-wide and had named their prices; and during another marathon meeting December 15, 1964, a half year behind schedule, the Council adopted common prices to take effect in 1967 that were very near the prices originally proposed by the Commission.

The Commission had next to formulate a scheme for financing farm subsidies. And, after studying anticipated costs and revenue, it came up with a plan for financing by income from agricultural and industrial tariffs, and that proposal precipitated the French boycott of the Common Market during the latter half of 1965. Immediately after the boycott began, the Eurocrats hurried to draft the kind of financing scheme (based on national contributions) France demanded, but the new proposal was not discussed by the Council until the end of the boycott in February 1966. Haggling over national contributions to the subsidies plan then occupied several Council meetings. Finally, with the Commission continuously available to offer new compromise solutions, at still another Council marathon May 11, 1966, contributions quotas were decided for the period up to 1970. At the same time, market organizations newly designed by the Eurocrats for certain crops were adopted, all-European prices for certain other crops were set, and a timetable for adopting regulations on still further crops was laid down. The creation of a common market in agriculture had by this time progressed to the point where it was possible to formulate the Community's position in the talks with non-membered nations on tariff disarmament that had been delayed while the Community figured out its new agricultural regime. So again, on the basis of painstaking preparation by the Eurocrats, on July 24, 1966, still another Council marathon resulted in agreement on a package solution to outstanding agricultural issues and an offer to be made by the Community in the Kennedy Round.

Thus went the continual and massive work of initiative. Throughout the history of Community farm legislation, other units of the administration were preparing new proposals in other fields, so that the Council at a meeting like the one in April, 1966, while struggling with agriculture, took action too, for instance, on liberalizing capital movements among the Six.

The work of the Eurocrats does not quite end with preparing proposals. They are forced to step a short distance over the line dividing them from direct administration. The Eurocrats *want* to step over the line, but that is beside the point. The Rome Treaty does not give the Commission enforcement, or police, powers. Institutions can reach all kinds of decisions as to what is right and proper under the Treaty, but they are not expected to administer those decisions directly with the public. The Rome Treaty leaves direct administration in the hands of national officials.

With the passage of time, however, the actions of the Commission have begun to take on some of the characteristics of administration. For one thing, economic regulations adopted by the law-making Council require centralized interpretation if they are to be consistent, and the Commission always falls heir to such tasks. Look, for example, at the actions of the Commission on March 2, 1966. The Commission took six decisions based on an authorization by the Council of April 4, 1962.[22] They all had to do with compensatory taxes that were to be levied upon goods provided to specific members of the Community by other members—goods like bread, cookies, caramels, and confections. And all of the decisions were in fact amendments to previous decisions of the Commission on the same subjects. What this type of decision amounted to was the detailed oversight of specific marketing situations by the Community, and that was direct administration. If the member governments had been permitted to determine the levies for themselves on the basis of *their* interpretation of the Council's decisions, then *they* would have been the implementers of the Council's policy. But it was not they; it was the Commission. Similar instances of direct administration grow more numerous as the Council continues to adopt policies that necessitate centralized oversight, and that is a growth that can continue indefinitely.

In the second place, the Commission falls increasingly into the role of umpire for disputes and complaints arising over the legislation of the Common Market, and in that role it is again an agency of direct administration, a kind of policeman. It assumes that role as a byproduct of a provision in the Rome Treaty that made court action by private parties unwieldy. Individuals have no access to the European Court unless they are challenging the validity of the actions of some Common Market organ. As far as normal en-

[22] *Journal officiel,* 9⁰ année, No. 58, 29 mars 1966.

forcement of the regulations is concerned, individuals are required to take their cases to *national* courts and to invoke the European Court's advice only if some problem of interpretation of a Community statute is involved. Final decisions are taken by the national courts, acting upon the European Court's advice if advice has been asked.

The Commission, however, *does* have direct access to the European Court,[23] and, if the Commission decides to pursue someone's grievance, it can bring offending national administrators to book in the European Court. Gentler forms of administrative intervention by the Commission, however, are usually enough to force an erring government back into line, but the gentle methods have been effective *because of* the Commission's formal power to take a case to court. The Commission might address an informal inquiry to the government concerned; and, if the Commission is not then satisfied by the way the regulations have been applied, it can render an official opinion to the government, requesting the necessary remedy. Only if the complaint is still not satisfied, would the case be taken to the European Court, whose decision is legally binding upon the member state involved.

Up to mid-1962 the Commission had received sixty-eight complaints against the way national administrations had applied regulations. So new was the problem of enforcement to the Common Market that at that time thirty of these had not yet been examined in any way, and sixteen of them were just being studied. That left twenty-two cases in which the Commission had actually acted as policeman. In twelve of them the offending administration made the necessary adjustment after the matter was called to its attention by the Commission. It was necessary to go a step farther and render an opinion in ten cases, but in only five of these did the offending administration then comply. The five most difficult cases had to be taken to court. Going to court was threat enough to make a national administration back down in one case, and the case was withdrawn. In two others, the European Court upheld the Commission, and the last two were still pending (in mid-1962).[24] The vol-

[23] *Traité instituant la Communauté économique européenne*, Art. 169.
[24] Emile Noël, Speech to Conservative Political Center, Oxford, England, July 7, 1962 [mimeographed].

ume of complaints grew steadily, and the Commission reported a worsening labor shortage in its legal staff. There were as many cases processed by the staff in 1965 as in the whole 1958 to 1962 period cited above, and the backlog of cases being studied had multiplied fourfold.[25]

The rule-making and enforcement responsibilities of the Eurocrats are an unavoidable outgrowth of the operation of the Community; they are not trumped up to promote European unity. They are a fact, not a campaign. Still there are widely differing attitudes toward direct administration by the Community. President de Gaulle of France was disturbed by the evolution. He said in his press conference of September 9, 1965, that the "international apparatus . . . often duplicated the competent national bureaus" and that the Eurocrats "abstained from excessive infringements" of the competence of national administrators.[26] In other words the Eurocrats *did* overstep though not excessively. His words were a warning.

President Hallstein was philosophical about the evolution of direct administration. He said to a British audience on March 25, 1965, "This procedure is . . . common to many federal systems, and is in keeping with their spirit." He wanted to allay fears that Community administrators would be "entirely cut off from the problems of each territory and [know] nothing of local practices or concerns." [27] Nothing Hallstein could say, however, allayed the fears of the national civil servants who looked upon the Brussels offices as a threat to their future and who constituted a permanent lobby against the Community bureaucracy. It is hard to be demoted from a sovereign to a subject administration, but would national administration suffice? Since each member had the job of paying to exporters the subsidies underwritten by the Common Market, for example, unscrupulous European traders were forging documents and collecting subsidies in several member countries on the *same* shipment. Community administration could cope with such problems better than national administration.

---

[25] Commission, *Neuvième rapport général*, p. 428.
[26] La Conférence de presse du Général de Gaulle, *Communauté européenne,* 9ᵉ année, octobre 1965, p. 9.
[27] The Commission, A New Factor in International Life, Address to the British Institute of International and Comparative Law, London, 25 March, 1965 [mimeographed].

Whether it is in its growth in policy-making power or growth in administrative responsibility that one measures the early achievements of the Commission, one can scarcely find a better example of political dynamism in the whole world of international organization. Officials of the Commission compared the tempo and spirit of their institution favorably with the United Nations Secretariat, for example, and the enthusiasm that prevailed in the corridors and offices of Brussels was a sign of healthy functioning. The demoralizing effect of the breakdown of negotiations over the admission of new members in 1963 proved a rude lesson for the Eurocrats, but there was no reason for the Common Market to lose momentum in the implementation of the treaty. It had only to accustom itself to the vicissitudes of international life, with spirits high one day over some new breakthrough in farm policy and low the next over the French boycott.

The Parliament

V

The European Parliament is an itinerant institution with three seats. It meets for one week per month in Strasbourg at the *Maison d'Europe,* the headquarters of an entirely separate organization, the Council of Europe. Here it lines the corridors with the trunks and packing cases in which it has to transport documents and clerical equipment every month from Luxembourg, which is the seat of the Parliament's secretariat. This monthly trek is the consuming problem of the secretariat, but it is powerless to do anything about it until the member governments select a permanent headquarters for the Community. Not only is the secretariat itinerant, the 142 members of Parliament have to travel from their six capital cities to Strasbourg every month likewise. At other times both the secretariat and the parliamentarians have to travel to the third seat, Brussels, for meetings of the Parliament's committees. Had Brussels been designated as the permanent capital of the Community, all of the Parliament's operation could have been moved there; but short of such a decision, Luxembourg and Strasbourg are too fond of their respective pieces of the Parliament to let go of them. The Parliament, in a sense, has inhabited those two cities for longer than the Common Market has been in Brussels, because the Schuman Plan assembly, the predecessor of the European Parliament, used the same facilities from 1952 to 1958.

The Power of Words

The Parliament is a strictly advisory body, and its influence is exerted chiefly upon the Council and the Commission, which give varying degrees of notice to its opinions. It cannot be otherwise until the Parliament uses its power to overturn the Commission or until the Treaty is amended to give the Parliament more power. On the other hand, the Parliament is buoyed up by the conviction that in due course it will become the legitimizing voice among the institutions of the United States of Europe. All the member nations are committed to the principle of parliamentary responsibility at home and that augurs well for the European Parliament. The lowly advisory role of the Parliament accounts for the awkwardness of its meeting arrangements, but its potential rise in station attracts proud and highly motivated officials to its chamber.

The *moral* superiority of a popularly based parliament was a clear principle of the Rome Treaty, as, indeed, it is of Western political philosophy generally. The European Parliament was treated first in the articles of the Treaty dealing with institutions of the Community, and in the annual reports of the Commission and the *Yearbook* of the Parliament the account of the activity of the Parliament is given precedence over the other Community institutions. Any conscious or unconscious divergences from the principle of parliamentary primacy are quickly protested by parliamentarians, as when the information service of the Community published a *Guide to the European Communities* in which the Commission was first in the order of discussion.

The principle of primacy was cultivated by the Parliament also by changing its name, which was expressed as the *Assembly* by the Rome Treaty. The Assembly first attached adjectives and went under the name of European Parliamentary Assembly for several years. Later, the adjective **Parliame**ntary was changed to a noun and the official word Assembly **was d**ropped altogether, giving the body the still more prestigious **name** *European Parliament*. Popular journals warmed up to the **new** name immediately, but the Commission's persistence in addressing the Parliament as the Assembly occasioned another outburst of stung pride in the Parliament which

settled the matter of the new name. Still, the Parliament could
only advise.

Who Speaks for Europe?

The European Parliament consists of members of national parliaments chosen by those parliaments in such a way as to reflect
the strengths of the various parties at home.[1] Seats are apportioned
so that France, Germany, and Italy have 36 each; Belgium and the
Netherlands, 14 each; and Luxembourg, 6. In order to allow the
national parliaments to devise their own methods of excluding
Communist and other extremist parliamentarians, there is no common method of election. In Belgium and Holland, where Communist representation in the national parliament is virtually nil,
and in Germany, where the Nazi and Communist parties are outlawed, the distribution of seats is determined by a proportional
party representation system; while in Italy and France, where there
are large Communist parties, the delegates to the European Parliament are chosen by majority vote from lists that distribute seats
among the moderate parties only. There are further minor national
variations in the method of selection, especially with respect to the
sharing of seats between the two houses in bicameral national parliaments. The exclusionary methods of election were defended on
the ground that the European Parliament was still too fragile and
undeveloped to absorb members other than those who were more
or less dedicated to the principles of European constitutionalism
and unity. But a price has been paid for the exclusions, because the
requisite majority cannot be mustered to elect a full delegation from
Italy. For eight years after the Rome Treaty, Western European
Communists echoed Soviet diatribes against the Common Market;
but, when polycentrism and revisionism emerged in international
communism, the French Communists turned around and made a
united front in 1965 with the French Socialists who strongly backed

[1] National methods for election of members of the European Parliament are
reviewed in Pierre Ginestet, *L'Assemblée parlementaire européenne*. Paris:
Presses Universitaire de France, 1959, pp. 73-78.

the Community. They then wanted representatives in the European Parliament, but they were still passed over.

The Rome Treaty envisaged the eventual election of the Parliament by direct suffrage and directed the Parliament to make a study of possible methods. The Parliament concluded its study[2] in 1960 by adopting a group of recommendations that amounted to a very cautious step toward a popular election system. They specified that, during a transition period,[3] the national parliaments would continue to choose one-third of the membership and that the membership of the parliament would be tripled. By this device no current parliamentarian would need to lose his seat. Also, should something go amiss in the direct election system, the one-third control of membership retained by the national parliaments would enable them to compensate through the make-up of their own national delegations. As for the two-thirds of the seats to be filled by direct election under the proposed system, parties ineligible for national parliamentary elections (i.e., the Nazis and Communists in Germany) were to be ineligible for the European Parliament; and each nation would follow its own election procedures during the transition period. *Europeanized* methods of election would be decided by Parliament later.

Some parliamentarians counted on the elections to help them achieve rapport with the voters at home, thus breathing new political strength into the Parliament. Others feared, however, that direct elections would produce a group of blindly elected nobodies, whose presence would lessen the political power of the European Parliament. There was no real fear of the possibility that Communists might win seats in the Parliament. Nor was there fear that the existing Parliament would lose efficiency with the 426 members proposed.

The proposal incorporated some common vices of electoral legislation. By reserving one-third of the seats for members who like themselves would be chosen by national parliaments, the parliamentarians were protecting their *own* seats in the European Parliament

[2] The study was widely published by the Parliament as *Vers l'élection direct de l'Assemblée parlementaire européenne.* Luxembourg, 1960.

[3] An indeterminate period (Art. 4, *Ibid.,* p. 70) to be ended by vote of the European Parliament.

and practically guaranteeing that the newcomers that ran for the remaining seats would be political nobodies. The proposal to triple the membership flew in the face of contemporary thought on legislative reform favoring smaller and better-staffed legislative bodies. There was a clear effort being made to cushion the step and thus to court approval by the Council of Ministers, such as by the provision that each country would follow its own election procedures temporarily. Still, the Council was not ready to expose the sheltered European Parliament to the political out of doors, and it pigeonholed the electoral proposal. Because of strong French opposition to an elected parliament, the prospects of favorable Council action were so dim that no further work was done on the proposal.[4]

The Parliament, therefore, has no popular mandate. The parliamentarians are representatives of national governments, albeit of the *parliaments* of national governments, and the Council reminds them of this by addressing them as representatives of governments. On the other hand, the Parliament is the most democratic institution of the Community. Its members are national politicians whose whole professional careers have been conditioned by the necessity of keeping the interests of their constituents in view. In Strasbourg they are politicians off duty in that they do not represent their constituents there; they represent parliaments. But they are not Dr. Jekylls at home and Mr. Hydes in Strasbourg. They are the same personalities in either place, motivated by the same political instincts and thinking in the same idioms.

Persons chosen to go to Strasbourg are committed to the cause of European unity and want to go. The average age of the members was fifty-seven in 1966, an age that was testimony to long national parliamentary experience and significant national standing.[5] There was strong representation of ages from fifty-five to sixty-five. Membership in the Parliament is a mark of distinction; and seats are sought competitively, with the consequence that the better established parliamentarians are the ones whose selection is assured. They

[4] A thorough survey of the precedents and other considerations that would bear on the system eventually formulated is by Wolfgang Birke, *European Elections by Direct Suffrage*. Leyden: A. W. Sythoff, 1961.

[5] Age data are from Parlement européen, *Annuaire 1965-1966*, Luxembourg, 1966, pp. 17-154.

bring to the institution the sense of parliamentary style to which they are already accustomed. Participation is out of the question for national party leaders, however, because they are too busy at home.

Ages range from thirty-four years to eighty-two years and embrace both the elder statesmen of Europe such as Gaetano Martino, Rene Pleven, Mario Scelba, or Pierre Pflimlin, who fathered the European communities or were at one time or another heads of government, and also some younger parliamentarians who see in the European Parliament a potential mainstream of European politics. The promise of the Parliament even sweeps up parliamentarians who have only a mild commitment to European unity but who consider that involvement with the European Parliament can be a wise move in their careers at home. On the other hand participation can cut so deeply into a member's time that he can damage his political standing at home. Successful participation in the Parliament attracts attention, and in 1965 one of its vice presidents was elevated by the Coal and Steel Community to membership on its executive board. Participation tends to become a habit, and the Parliament has become identified with specific individuals. The average age of the group rises, therefore, as the standbys grow older.[6] The Parliament would have to have had more success sooner if it were going to grow younger.

Looking the Part

Strasbourg is alive with sessions of the Parliament for about one week each month, except for the holiday seasons of Christmas, Easter, and summer.[7] By starting early on Monday morning and devoting every morning, afternoon, and evening to the work of the Parliament, the delegates can finish their business on Thursday, or Wednesday evening at the earliest. The expenses of the delegates are borne by the Parliament, so that no delegate is under financial strain in being a member. He is under the strain, however, of

[6] The average age rose from 56 in 1961 to 58 in 1965, but fell to 57 in 1966.
[7] Once a year it holds a joint meeting with the Consultative Assembly of the Council of Europe to discuss the condition of Europe.

holding seats in two parliaments, both of which deserve full time. That has been his most immediate rationale for wanting the direct election of members to serve in the European Parliament alone. The parliamentarians complain ceaselessly about the practical impossibility of doing justice to both their national and European parliamentary duties. The city of Strasbourg is an ideal locale for this sort of high-pressure work, because it offers few diversions.

At the *Maison d'Europe,* delegates pass a Strasbourg police honor guard as elaborate as that to which the national houses of parliament are accustomed and enter a meeting hall that is a temporary structure already beginning to show signs of dilapidation. There they distribute their time among the floor of the Parliament, committee rooms, and the restaurant. All three places are important. The committee meetings are secret, but they discuss technical matters of little interest to the general public, usually questions raised by the Commission and Council. Committee rooms are also the scene of meetings of the European political groups, or parties, that form within the Parliament and define shades of opinion on the issues of the day to be aired on the floor or for the press.[8] The attempt to weld various national party members into international parliamentary parties is only partially successful, and often consensus is difficult to achieve within the groups. All parties are in favor of European unity, however, and so proposals touching close to the subject of unity are bound to have enthusiastic backing from all sides; and debate is used mainly for exhortation and emphasis. Like the tea terrace of the British House of Commons, the restaurant doubles as the parliamentarian's office, consultation room, rendezvous point, and rest haven.

Much more than in a national parliament, the debates on the floor of the European Parliament are the center of interest to both the parliamentarians and the public. Although Strasbourg cannot provide the meetings of the Parliament with the profusion of tourist observers that New York cascades upon the United Nations, the organization of classes and groups to visit meetings of Parliament prove the work of that body to be a vital and moving experience for many Europeans. Reporters are present, who, for want of experience, sometimes issue poor dispatches but nevertheless bring the

[8] They are dealt with in the next chapter.

Parliament in headlines and photographs to more Europeans than does any other medium. The members of the Commission all attend regularly, and once or twice a year the members of the Council of Ministers attend. The Parliament wanted the Council at every session but accepted the promise of occasional attendance in order to avoid being sent substitutes.[9] It is here in the plenary meetings that the institution sees itself as a parliament, seated in an earnest and austere amphitheater with liveried ushers and with the kaleidoscopic circulation of personalities and opinions that characterize assemblies of men concerned with decisions of state. And it is here that the great causes can be expounded.

It takes more than an auditorium to make a Parliament, however, and what sets the tone of the *Maison d'Europe* is above all the sincere and energetic way in which the European parliamentarians pursue their duties in Strasbourg. What makes them run? Idealism motivates the parliamentarians, but, too, their behavior is conditioned by the hierarchy of offices of their institution. With a record of industry and intelligence in the Parliament, a younger member can hope to find an office in the hierarchy at, perhaps, the committee level and thus derive the satisfaction that rewards success in competition. It was alleged that the European parliamentary group called the *Liberals* had no political homogeniety and existed mainly to create more Parliamentary offices. Members of the Liberal group contested this allegation, but the fact remains that there are approximately half as many offices in the Parliament as there are seats! Not as many as half of the parliamentarians are office-holders, however, because certain of the key leaders hold several posts.

Competition for the presidency has set the political tone of the Parliament. Except in an honorific sense, the office of president does not carry with it much political status. Even in arranging the order of business of the Parliament, the president has to defer to committees. An attempt has been made to endow the office with prestige by electing European leaders of highest standing in the movement for unity, as was the custom of the Common Assembly of the Schuman Plan, the predecessor of the European Parliament. The election of Robert Schuman, the late French minister and

[9] P.-H. J. M. Houben, *Les Conseils de Ministres des Communautés Européennes.* Leyden: A. W. Sythoff, 1964, p. 163.

author of the Schuman Plan, lent distinction to the office during the first years of the new Parliament, 1958 to 1960. Moreover, the president is the natural spokesman for the Parliament; and, when he is working to enlarge the role of the Parliament in Community affairs, he can count on the solid support of all factions of the Parliament, as when he conferred with the presidents of all the national parliaments in 1963 on strategies for increasing parliamentary impact on European affairs. Still there was no talk of a contest over the office until 1962. Robert Schuman served for two annual terms by reason of a gentleman's agreement that each president would be reelected once. The liquidation of the Schuman Plan Assembly had interrupted the term of Hans Furler, who was compensated by election for two terms as president of the new Parliament following Schuman.

In 1962, the Christian Democratic group made up nearly half of all the members of the Parliament, and Schuman and Furler, had both been from that group. The Christian Democrats contended that as long as theirs was the largest party in the Parliament they ought to be allowed to elect one of their number as president, and even the Socialists, the second largest party, assumed that they could not stop them. For a while the healthy air of normal partisan competition pervaded the atmosphere of the Parliament. In the end, however, other considerations prevailed. The Parliament elected by secret ballot Gaetano Martino, not a Christian Democrat, but a member of the weak Liberal group. His special qualification for the office was that he ranked among the earliest and most diligent fathers of European unity and especially of the Common Market, since it was at a meeting at his home in Messina that the plan for the Common Market was rescued in 1955. Secondly, he was Italian, which affected a geographic rotation of the office, the two previous presidents having been French (Schuman) and German (Furler).

The temptation of the political groups to view the election in partisan terms became irresistible in 1964, and a senior Belgian member of the Christian Democratic group, Jean Duvieusart, was elected in a real contest, fifty-seven votes to fifty-one. He was unable to complete his second term because he did not seek reelection to the Belgian Senate, and another Belgian Christian Democratic group member, Victor Leemans, was elected unopposed to complete the term. At the next regular election in 1966 the French Christian Democratic group leader Alain Poher won the presidency, seventy-three votes to forty-one.

The Socialists, if they were ever going to have the presidency, would have to earn it by increasing their numbers in Strasbourg; and they would have to earn those seats by winning larger votes in national elections. The Parliament was beginning to take itself seriously, and it was about time. For, if it did not, nobody else would. The Parliament had to choose between the luxury of an honorific president, devoted entirely to fairness and good order in the prosecution of parliamentary business, and an aggressive president capable of extraordinary tactics and inch-by-inch aggrandizement to revise the constitutional order that brought the Parliament into existence in such low estate.

Although the avenues to the presidency do not lie open to the average member of Parliament, faithful work within the institution can be rewarded in other ways. There is the possibility to become chairman of one of the committees of Parliament, of which there are thirteen, or to be rapporteur for a committee on some specific topic. Publicity for committee action usually bears the name of the key persons involved. A parliamentarian's satisfaction with life in Strasbourg depends a great deal, too, upon what committee he is on, because some committees are more interesting than others. The most important committee is the Political Committee, which heads the Parliament's campaign for a stronger voice in the Community. The Agriculture Committee comes next, because of the hot debates over agricultural policy in the Community. As to third rank it is difficult to differentiate the Committee on the Internal Market and Committee on Economics and Finance as to importance; but they stand out above other committees. The coveted committee posts have to be won by subtle methods of parliamentary competition.

The Parliament operates smoothly and fruitfully by habit, because its procedure departs very little from that to which the parliamentarians are accustomed at home in their national parliaments.[10] Parliamentary procedures follow more or less the same

[10] An exhaustive treatise on procedures of the European Parliament is Henri Manzanares, *le Parlement européen*. Paris: Editions Berger-Levrault, 1964. The rules of procedure of the Parliament are often amended, and the current version is published annually in the *Annuaire* of the Parliament.

general pattern throughout Western Europe and are based on the early parliamentary democracy in France, which spread elsewhere in Europe as monarchial governments gave way to republics. The Parliament's household is managed by the *Bureau* (office), which meets biweekly and is composed of the president and eight vice presidents—distributed among nationalities and political groups— who are elected by the Parliament. The *Bureau* chooses and supervises the Parliament's secretary general and assigns parliamentarians to committees subject to approval by the whole Parliament. The agenda of the Parliament is decided upon by yet another body, the Committee of Presidents, which is larger and consists of some two dozen key officers of the Parliament, its committees, and its political groups. It meets just once at each of the monthly sessions of Parliament in order to arrange the agenda for the following month.

The president has to abide by the decisions of these top-level bodies, but he exerts personal influence over the Parliament because of the natural need of such a complex institution for one person, like a traffic cop, to mesh together its endeavors. The president may consult the various committee and political-group leaders, but in the end he may have to run rough shod over some of their wishes, for instance, by setting arbitrary time limits for debate. These or any other rulings of the president are subject to parliamentary approval, but he can count on the support of the house for honest efforts to cut through the tangle of procedural interests at play in the chamber. The work of organizing the debate keeps the president *away* from the debate most of the time, and the honor of holding the gavel is passed through the hands of many temporary presidents in the course of a session.

What the president sees facing him in the chamber are the political groups with seating organized like slices of a pie, the segments from left to right being filled by Socialists, Christian Democrats, Liberals, and Gaullists. The group leaders sit in front. Speeches are long, but to the point. A sitting might start out with a long report by a member of one of the executives from Brussels or Luxembourg followed by an equally long discussion of it by political group leaders and possibly a comment or two from backbenchers. All speakers stand in their places; and, since the leaders down front do most of the talking, the average parliamentarian looks at the back of a speaker. When a committee report is debated, it might be introduced by an hour-long speech by the rapporteur concerned, followed by forty-minute-long speeches from each of the group leaders and fifteen-minute speeches by backbenchers. A day's sitting begins at 10:30 or 11:00 A.M. and lasts until 8:30 or 9:00 P.M. with no recess, during which time a total of about twenty persons can speak from one to sixty minutes each. Since the Parliament gauges its success by the number of issues it draws into debate, it deliberates on one, two, or even three new subjects every day, each subject being broached by the rapporteur's long speech followed by the long commentaries by the leadership. Often the reports or commentaries are prepared with special care with a view to their later publication in pamphlets or journals other than the official documents of the sessions. Speakers consider the public to which they are talking to be far wider than that within the walls of the *Maison d'Europe*.

The Rome Treaty allowed parliamentarians to address questions to the executive commissions.[11] Although the Treaty did not envisage questioning the Council of Ministers, that body honored the Parliament with answers of some sort to the few questions addressed to it. Most questions, however, have been directed to the Commission of the Common Market, and all but a few have been written questions concerning actions the parliamentarians thought were not quite right. The written question has a special impact in that it is newsworthy when it is posed as well as when it is answered, and it is published in the *Official Journal* of the Community along with the lawmaking decisions of other organs. Starting with 30 written questions in 1958, the annual crop grew to almost 200 in 1963 but fell back to 136 by 1965.[12] Questions are apt to be written by Dutchmen (half of all questions)[13] and in particular by a Mr. Vredeling, who was author of one-fourth of all 1965 questions. In connection with certain Dutch tulip-marketing controls he asked, for instance, why the Commission had not proposed a common

[11] Communauté économique européenne, *Traité instituant la Communauté économique européenne et documents annexes*. Bruxelles, 1957, Art. 140.
[12] Based on listings in the *Annuaire* of the Parliament. Only questions answered in the given year are counted.
[13] Houben, *op. cit.*, p. 173.

tulip market; and the Commission answered that it was *going* to.[14]
Questions were often of this nature.

Informal oral questions might come up in debate and might be
answered immediately by a commissioner or later in the day or
the following day after some inquiry into the matter. There exists
also a procedure for posing formal oral questions; but, since that
entails long advanced notice to the parties questioned and also a
struggle to get time on the agenda for an answer, the procedure is
almost never used. The posing and answering of an oral question
is too challenging a confrontation for the continental parliamentarian. They lack the Englishman's ability to ask or retort to heck-
ling questions, and they habitually avoid proceedings of the sort
that border on conversation or argument. When full dress debate
was staged October 21, 1964, on an oral question, one group leader
decried the use of the questioning procedure for propaganda purposes.[15] The Parliament seemed determined to have a toothless oral
questioning procedure.

The Parliament completed its procedural paraphernalia by making provision for petitions from the public.[16] Since it has received
petitions at the average rate of one every two years since 1952
when the Schuman Plan assembly instituted the practice, each
one has drawn special attention, as did the appeal in 1964 from
the municipal council of Saint Savin, a charming town in Poitou
that is world famous for its Romanesque church and ancient
frescos. The council wanted the creation of a single European
currency.

As in other modern parliaments, the preparatory work for general
debates is done in closed committee meetings. The life of the committees is somewhat detached from the Parliament because their
meetings are usually held in Brussels *between* the monthly parliamentary sessions. Issues are assigned to committees by the Parliament, but a committee can take up matters on its own. It is never
certain what session the Parliament will be able to devote to a
committee's report, because there are always more reports in prep-

[14] Questions écrites avec réponses, No. 132 de M. Vredeling a la Commission
de la C.E.E., *Journal officiel*, 8ᵉ année, No. 45, 19 mars 1965, pp. 683-684.

[15] Parlement européen, *Débats*, Session 1964-1965, Séances du 19 au 23 octobre
1964, pp. 116-117.

[16] Rules of Procedure, Article 47 (*Annuaire 1964-1965*, p. 288).

aration than the Parliament can bring to the floor for extensive debate.

Following the continental tradition, each committee has competence over one field of subject matter, such as agriculture, transport, or social affairs. And, since the eight large committees have twenty-nine members each (five small ones have seventeen each) it is necessary for each parliamentarian to be a member of three committees, with no guarantee that their meetings will be rationally spaced. During one month an Italian parliamentarian, for instance, might have a week of meetings in Strasbourg and another eight days, possibly scattered, of committee meetings in Brussels, after each of which he has to return to Rome to attend his own parliament.

Committee work can be interesting for the parliamentarian, because testimony from the Commission in Brussels brings them as close as they ever come to understanding the technical background of issues on which they are preparing reports. That places the committees very much at the mercy of the information provided by the Commission, but in Brussels the parliamentarians feel closest to the actual policy-making process of the Community. One or two committee meetings are held at Commission headquarters every day, and the continual contacts with committees make it impossible for a commissioner to treat their opinions slightingly without poisoning his long-term relationship with the groups. The Commission wants to compare its notions born of cloistered reasoning and consultation at headquarters with the broad spread of opinion and popular representation found in the Parliament. And, too, whatever influence the Parliament has in national capitals, the Commission wants to enlist in its dealings with the Council. So it has to pay a price by accepting some planning ideas initiated by the parliamentarians, such as the Parliament's demand for greater budgetary powers, which was made part of the celebrated Commission proposal in 1965 that caused the French boycott. But the Commission knows it can treat the Parliament with polite firmness and rely on a backlog of tolerance and enthusiasm.

The Parliament had an "invisible" secretariat of 483 in 1966. Its headquarters is in Luxembourg, but it is customarily not at home, what with the continual meetings in Strasbourg and Brussels.

Its life is the most bizarre of all those affected by the lack of a permanent headquarters for the Community. The secretary general of the Parliament, unlike the secretary general of the United Nations, is not the central personality of the Parliament but rather its chief clerk responsible for providing facilities for meetings and printing documents. One secretary general who had illusions about his status was forced to resign.

The secretariat watches the progress of the committees so as to be able to bring to completion a half-dozen or so reports around a single theme for each of the monthly sessions, and their thematic plan is handed over to the Committee of Presidents of the Parliament for adoption as the provisional agenda of the following session. Even the the most careful planning can go awry, however, because the Rome Treaty provided for the consultation of Parliament by the Commission and such consultations can come up at any time, depending on the Commission's rather than the Parliament's rhythm of work.

The secretariat also has to cope with tight budgetary limits set by the Council of Ministers. The Parliament does not grow, so why should it need more money? Thus if the Parliament needs money to finance an increased number of committee meetings it has to tighten its budget for documents. The documentation budget is a sensitive question, because the Parliament is not so much a decision-making body as a propaganda machine; and it needs vasts amounts of publicity. It publishes more documents than all the rest of the institutions put together, in more languages, and disseminates them more widely, mostly free. The object of the propaganda ultimately is to share the powers of the Council, which, in turn, has hold of the purse strings governing the propaganda effort—a neat deadlock, adding intensity to Parliament's effort to gain budgetary powers.

The Politics of Harassment

The Parliament has not exercised control over the other institutions of the Community. Its impotence is self-imposed, as explained above, because it does not wish to use its power to fire the

Commission. It is better to wait until the Community develops far enough for the Commission to be *worth* firing. The Parliament examines the Commission's proposals critically, but the relationship between the two organs is characterized by mutual assistance. The Commission values the endorsement and assistance of the Parliament. Commissioner Lemaignen credited the German chairman of the Parliament's committee on overseas territories with frequent intercessions in Bonn to aid the Commission.[17] For its part the Parliament wants to fatten the Commission the way the witch in the candy house in the forest was trying to fatten Hansel. The Rome Treaty made the Commission responsible to the Parliament, and eventually all its powers would be under the Parliament's influence.

Relations with the Council are another matter. The Parliament has no direct leverage for the Council. It can only harass the Council with resolutions, manifestos, questions, visitations, conferences, propaganda, and lobbying in home capitals. Its demands take little notice of the Council's concern for the welfare of the Community or the limitations on the personal power of Council members. A Council member feels as much at home at meetings of the Parliament as a politician would at a conference of the opposition party.

The Rome Treaty required the Council to consult the Parliament on twenty different types of decisions, but how should it consult a body whose advice it need not take? The Council was conscious of its sovereign self-sufficiency, but it was divided as to what it should do to make the Parliament feel involved and important in European policy-making. It decided that new proposals of the Commission should be passed on immediately to the Parliament by the Council, that the Parliament should make known its advice by resolution, and that direct contact should be made at annual or semiannual meetings of the Council with Parliament. The *pro forma* referral of new proposals has worked fairly smoothly except that sometimes ministers have insisted that there be a preliminary exchange of views in the Council so as to give the Parliament guidance and prevent it from rambling over political ground where it need not tread. The Parliament's resolutions are distributed to the Council members when received, "taken note of" by the Council, and probably left unread by the busier ministers. The Council

[17] Robert Lemaignen, *L'Europe au Berceau.* Paris: Plom, 1964, p. 155.

attempts to give the Parliament reasons when it overrules its advice, but it has often been remiss in this respect. The productivity of the Parliament is too great, and the Council's interest in the Parliament too small.

Moreover, the Council decided that, when in doubt, parliamentary consultation was to be considered as *not* required. For instance, when taking up a proposal by the Commission on criteria for the establishment of minimum prices, the Council had to cope with the fact that the Treaty required consultation with the Parliament. It so happened, however, that the Parliament had already adopted a resolution relating to the question, and so the president of the Council ruled that referral of the proposal to the Parliament would not be necessary unless the Council were going to insert some new ideas into the measure.

When the Parliament is especially concerned about the Council, it sends a delegation of parliamentary officers to speak to it, such as the group that spoke on behalf of an amendment to increase appropriations for the Parliament. In this case, although the Council rejected other amendments the Parliament had proposed, it did increase the funds of the Parliament as requested. The relationship between the Parliament and the Council was not so distant, in other words, that the Council would allow the Parliament to become poverty stricken. But the most careful and personal approaches by the Parliament to the Council give no guarantee that pleas will be granted, as was illustrated by the Council's shelving the Parliament's plan for direct elections. The recalcitrance of the Council does not imply antidemocratic or anticommunitarian feeling in the body. The Council could be fully in favor of the Common Market and still coolly jealous of its authority to make decisions for the organization. When has a policy-making body shared authority, even in a democracy, without being required constitutionally to do so?

The Council is subject to indirect pressure by the Parliament. A prime example was the time the Parliament stole the initiative in negotiating with the former French empire in Africa. While the Parliament's action was pending, the Council tried unsuccessfully to move in to control its timing and effect. But by the time the Council came around to negotiating and adopting the terms of association with the African states, the principles had already been shaped in discussions with the Africans at a conference sponsored by the Parliament in Rome, and the Council chafed under the pressure. The Parliament's gesture toward the Africans was brilliant in several respects. With generous assistance from the Italian government the conference feted the African leaders sumptuously and made them feel important—equal to their European counterparts. The two sides communicated in a profound sense, as testified the enthusiastic involvement of one African statesman, who took over the interpretation of German-French and French-German when one of the hired European interpreters was indisposed. Among other things, the Parliament arranged to meet every year with African parliamentarians and thus have a continuing voice in the association.

Council members are quick to point out that they were bound by instructions from governments and that, if the Parliamentarians would get busy at home, they might get those instructions changed. Work at home, fine! But on whom? The votes of the Council are secret and instructions to Council members are secret, and so Parliamentarians normally do not know whether their home government is erring or not, either during consideration of a matter or after a decision is taken. Celebrated issues and antagonists cannot be concealed. The Dutch and Italian governments allowed their positions favoring the direct election of the Parliament to be published.[18] But relations between the Council and the home parliaments are feeble, consisting normally of annual reports to parliaments on the activities of the Community, which might or might not be debated. Or the Community might come up once a year as one of many items of expenditure in the national budget and be debated with the rest. Only the Belgian parliament has a committee devoted to European affairs.

National parliaments in France, Germany, and the Netherlands have criticized their representatives in the Council occasionally. On June 13, 1962 a majority of the members of the French National Assembly wished to reject a foreign policy speech just delivered in the Chamber by the foreign minister and to adopt a resolution favoring European union. But in order to avoid overthrowing the

[18] Houben, *op. cit.*, p. 191.

government by their action they filed out into the corridor to cast their vote unofficially. This curious action illustrates a dilemma of European parliamentarians. Most of them are members of majority parties in the national capitals and owe their political lives to the same political leadership that hands instructions to the members of the Council. How could they exert *pressure* on such men? They are not likely to pass any motion of nonconfidence and turn out their own leaders and party from office. It was easy enough to pass resolutions in home parliaments *supporting* the home government and indirectly opposing some other government, like the German and Dutch parliamentary resolutions to refuse ratification to any new financing schemes for the Community that did not confer real budgetary powers on the European Parliament. But such actions had no direct influence on the French, for example, who were against giving powers to the European Parliament.

In short, the Parliamentarians do not have a grip on Community policy anywhere. Strasbourg and the home capitals are merely different arenas from which to influence the Council and Commission and to appeal to the citizenry of Europe—to attempt to orient parties, pressure groups, and public opinion to the uniting of Europe.

Political Forces

VI

When one spoke of European political forces during past decades, one ordinarily referred to subjective forces, such as nationalism, romanticism, or imperialism; but times have changed. After the creation of the Common Market, tangible political forces emerged on the European scene in the form of political parties, pressure groups, and expressions of public opinion. A good gauge of the progress of the European Community is the degree to which the politics of Europe have reoriented from their traditional national framework to the wider framework of the Common Market. There is no fooling politicians or lobbyists, who are quick to discover where decisions are *really* being made and where political power is shifting.

Euro-parties[1]

The European Parliament is a crucible in which national parties are being fused into European parties, a process whose success is more apparent than real. When the forerunner of the Parliament, the Schuman Plan assembly, first met, it split up the national delegations in its membership by seating members alphabetically instead of by nationality but assigned committe posts along strict national lines. Later the whole picture shifted, and national lines

[1] Treated at length in Guy van Oudenhove, *The Political Parties in the European Parliament.* Leyden: A. W. Sythoff, 1965.

of organization gave way to party lines that cut across nationality. After 1955 the committees were made up according to the relative strengths of party groups with equitable attention to national distribution only when feasible, and in the plenary meetings members were seated by party groups. The European Parliament perpetuated this system.

European parties were not wholly the creatures of the European Parliament. Even before the Schuman Plan the national Christian Democratic parties had a nexus in the Catholic church, and the national Social Democratic parties in the Socialist International. Hence, some impetus to form European parties within the institutions of the Community existed from the start.

Several parties emerged in the European Parliament, each of which had at least the fourteen-member minimum for party status under the rules of the Parliament. In 1966 there was a Christian Democratic Party[2] with sixty-one members, a Socialist Party with thirty-five, a Liberal Party with twenty-six, and a European Democratic Union Party consisting of fifteen French Gaullists, some of whom had belonged to the Liberal Party before their new party was created in 1965. Except for the Gaullists splintering off from the Liberals, party numbers changed very little from year to year.

The ideological tendencies of the parties is a projection of their national counterparts. The Socialists watch out for the interests of industrial workers in particular and urge increasing amounts of public participation in planning, financing, and managing the economy. The Christian Democrats are more moderate in pursuing very similar goals. The Liberals are *laissez-faire* politicians and resist the uniting of Europe by means of unnecessary regulations trumped up for the purpose, but they are no less dedicated to European unity. The Gaullists insist on a national party of their own and are defensive about De Gaulle's posture of diplomatic isolation and his concept of Europe as a "union of fatherlands," but they go to Strasbourg because they are interested in the uniting of Europe. They view the more avid support for European unity

[2] Although the rules use the French term *groupe* (Art. 36), that term was inspired by the practice of calling a political formation in a national parliament a *groupe*. In the English language, formations in a parliament are called *parties*.

among the other parties as pretense. Both the Christian Democrats
and the Socialists hope to profit politically from European unity.
A union of the Six would make the Christian Democrats the
largest party indefinitely; but, from the Socialist point of view, the
next step would be the admission of Great Britain and Scandinavia,
both of which have strong Socialist parties. Even before then the
Christian Democrats could lead by coalition only.

The parties, other than the purely French Gaullist party, have
members from all over the Community. The Socialist Party is the
most cohesive group; and, although the Christian Democrats claim
to be just as cohesive, they are probably somewhat behind the
Socialists. Liberals, because they do not all originate from so-called
"liberal" parties at home, do not claim a high degree of cohesion
but assert that the other parties have little cohesion themselves.
In a sense, the Liberals are correct in that there are few means
of assuring party discipline; but they do not take adequately into
account the common outlook of, say, the members of the Socialist
Party. Except for the Gaullists, national delegations never meet
together for the transaction of business, albeit that there is natural
comradeship among compatriots and occasionally a national delegation may get together to act as host for an entertainment.

The work of each party revolves around the party leader, who is
chosen by his group and is assured of continuous tenure. The leaders
rose to prominence, they say, through seniority; they have been with
the Parliament since the beginning. But it is equally clear that
those men and women[3] exude the qualities of leadership that
would advance them in any arena of social or political competition.
Their responsibilities are as demanding as those of any national
parliamentary leader. On the days of sittings they hold early morning meetings with their parties to map out positions and strategies
on issues. After a plenary sitting begins, the leaders have to be in
two places at once—in their seats at the front of the chamber to
deliver long commentaries on topics under debate and also in their
offices to speak to the press, visitors, fellow party members, and

[3] Miss Käte Strobel (West Germany) became the Socialist leader after the
previous leader, Mr. Birkelbach (West Germany), left the European Parliament
in 1964.

parliamentary officers responsible for the organization of the debate. The party leaders' offices and small staffs are furnished by the Parliament.

The Europeanization of party politics is being accomplished in other ways as well. Both the national Christian Democratic parties and the national Social Democratic parties hold occassional international meetings to exchange views on issues of common European concern. There is an organization of the Socialist parties of the Community that has its own liaison bureau at the secretariat offices of the Parliament; and the parliamentary parties try to reach the general public by publishing press releases on European issues. On the other hand, partisan organization has not yet begun to affect the other institutions of the European Community. The Council of Ministers represents national interests rather than partisan interests, and the Commission always maintains a united front, although there are both Socialist and Christian Democratic commissioners.

The parties of the Parliament cannot afford to be strictly partisan in all matters. The four parties are but branches of one movement, the movement for European integration, which is the big wheel in which the small wheels of the parliamentary parties turn. Although clear disagreements between the parties are expressed on the floor of the Parliament, any proposal that provokes serious criticism is withdrawn for further study. Resolutions are often adopted by what the Parliament describes as unanimity or quasi-unanimity. There is lacking, therefore, any strong motivation for party discipline, and members feel free to express views that diverge from the stand of their parties. The parties have the power to expel members, but such action is only a remote possibility.

The seed of party politics will take root and blossom only when European issues are brought to the public through parliamentary campaigns and elections in which the practicing parliamentarians are forced to compete with candidates whose interests might be quite different from theirs, including some that oppose European integration. The practice of limited partisanship, however, can bear fruit too. Some leaders have seniority in the Parliament dating back to 1952 and could serve as elder statesmen around whom the more solidly based parties of the future might form. And the existing parties are already building traditions of doctrine and organization that would fit them for real responsibility if the Parliament enlarged its powers.

Euro-pressure Groups

Wherever decisions of political importance are being made, there one will find pressure groups. It is awkward to use this term in describing the pressures surrounding the Common Market, because despite academic research in Europe on pressure groups, the term carries a stigma there.

The foremost European pressure group has been the European Movement, a large private federation of national and international societies dedicated to the promotion of European unity. It has held a special position partly because it helped promote the establishment of the European Community and partly because its highly placed members found their way into offices of the new Community and offices of member governments. The movement has not attempted to exert influence on specific policy problems of the Community. It is concerned primarily with coordinating secondary forms of pressure exerted by conferences, public information, and other forms of publicity. Integrationist pressure has been spearheaded by a newer (1955) and smaller (forty members) group headed by one of the guiding spirits of the Schuman Plan Treaty, Jean Monnet, and consisting of pro-European leaders of all the major parties and labor federations of the Common Market nations. This group, known as the *Action Committee for a United States of Europe,* made its debut in the fight for ratification of the Rome treaties, and its function is to lobby in the capitals in support of new moves to further European integration.

Each advance toward the objective of European unity gives increased strength to these groups, but ultimate success promises to make them as obsolete in Europe as the Federalist Party became in its day of victory in the United States. There is a new and different pattern of pressure politics in the Community that is replacing them. Groups interested in the day by day flow of policy of the Community appear wherever Community institutions are at work. Even in the lobbies of the Parliament's *Maison d'Europe,* where the least decisive actions are constitutionally possible, the representatives of business interests attend "to provide information for the guidance of the delegates." Representatives of coal and oil interests were on hand, for example, when the Parliament debated the power policy of the Community.

When the Schuman Plan began in 1952, it incorporated the French practice of "fuctional representation" in the form of a Consultative Council that mirrored the French government's Economic and Social Council. The Council institutionalized the lobbying activities of producers, laborers, and consumers groups in the Coal and Steel Community by giving each a seat in what was, in effect, an organ of the Community. Thus legitimized from the start, these interest groups established permanent offices next to the Community headquarters in Luxembourg and took part regularly in the rounds of consultations that preceded each step taken by the Community. It was just as important for the ECSC to maintain a close relationship with these lobbying groups as it was for the American Interstate Commerce Commission to work closely with the railroads, being mindful, of course, of the dangers of too close an association. A counterpart of the Consultative Council of the ECSC was included in the Common Market under the name of the Economic and Social Committee. One president of the French Economic and Social Council was made president of the Common Market's Economic and Social Committee, which carried the parallel between the two bodies to a fine point.

The committee has a large membership of one hundred and one elected by the Council, which is required by the Treaty to consult the committee concerning eleven different types of decisions. The Commission also poses questions to the committee. The committee plays less of a political role in determining policy than a technical role in informing the appropriate decision makers of popular and professional thought on a subject at issue. The political edges of the committee are smoothed off by the fact that it has to reach conclusions in only general terms since it meets no oftener than the Council itself. Politics are also removed from the election of the committee by gentleman's agreement. Its members are nominated directly by the governments, each of which has a quota of seats[4] weighted very much as are the Council's votes. The Rome Treaty[5] required the governments to nominate twice as many persons as their allotted seats in order to give the Council a choice, but the embarrassment with which this system threatened the loser is avoided by the Council, which votes unanimously for the names placed first on the lists. The remaining names normally appear first the next time there is an election.

The Economic and Social Committee exists because its advice is valued, but it is difficult to pin down what the value is. It is apt to approve propositions put before it, and it avoids controversy. And the *real* work of lobbying seems to go on as usual outside the framework of the committee.

By 1964 a total of some 233 different organizations[6] concerned with numerous special aspects of private and economic life had been established to deal with the Common Market, and about half of them had set up offices near the Common Market headquarters in Brussels, at their own expense and on their own initiative. The list of their names reads like the roster of lobbying organizations published in the American *Congressional Record*—The Association for the Coffee Trade and Industry in the EEC, The Banking Federation of the EEC, The Common Market Opticians Group, to name but a few. Even Italy's Communist-led labor union, the C.G.I.L., opened a Brussels office in 1963 as a revisionist gesture, but both it and the Communist-led C.G.T. in France failed in a bid for seats on the Economic and Social Committee in 1966.

Decisions of the Common Market are eventually going to affect the interests of *all* business, labor, professional, and consumers organizations in Europe. Let us examine the situation confronted by the Brussels lobby of the General Council on European Cinematographic Production. The European movie industry was in a serious state of decline as a result of competition from American films, from European television, and from other forms of entertain-

[4] France, Germany, and Italy 24 each; Belgium and the Netherlands 12 each; and Luxembourg 5.

[5] Communauté économique européenne, *Traité instituant la Communauté économique européenne et documents annexes.* Bruxelles, 1957, Art. 195.

[6] This figure is the total of listings by the Union of International Associations *op. cit.* The Community catalogued 140 the same year (*Communauté européenne,* 8ᵉ année, No. 10, octobre 1964, p. 16).

ment that Europeans could not afford earlier, such as weekends in the country. The European governments subsidized the film industry, but with widely varying methods that were in serious need of harmonization by the Common Market. The movie producers were interested in a cinematographic common market because they hoped to film high-budget movies that could match the American movie industry. Hollywood had access to the huge internal American market, and the European film makers wanted a market as big. *Better* films could result as well from such strengthening of the film industry, which would help it stave off the incursions of alternative forms of entertainment.[7] On the other hand, the ideas detailed to the European Commission by this group do not coincide with those of other organizations in Brussels such as the International Television Co-ordination Center (Eurovision), their archcompetitor.

The Brussels lobbies vary widely in size and importance. Among the important ones is the Union of Industries of the European Community, whose purpose is to establish the joint attitude of European industry on issues before the Common Market and to present it to the Community. The concerns of such a body are vast, and so it has more than one seat in the Economic and Social Committee. One of its representatives has been vice president of the committee.

The larger lobbies operate in a variety of methods. Eurosyndicat, for example, the Organization of Free Trade Unions of the EEC, has a secretariat in Brussels that maintains continual contact with the Common Market.[8] About one-quarter of the members of the Economic and Social Committee are affiliated with this organization. When the organization reaches a stand on some fundamental issue of the Community, it pursues it on a broad front. In 1959 it formulated a European Statute (of rights) for Miners, which was of particular concern to the Coal and Steel Community. The draft statute was promoted not only through the institutional channel

[7] Cf. Claude Degond, *Les Industries cinématographic des 'Six' et le Marché Commun, La Documentation Française.* Paris, 1966.
[8] The complicated interrelationships and levels of organization in the European labor movement are outlined in R. Colin Beever, *European Unity and the Trade Union Movement.* Leyden: Sythoff, 1960, Chap. 12.

of the ECSC Consultative Council but also in representations to the High Authority of the ECSC and to the relevant committee of the European Parliament. In conjunction with this effort, copies of the draft statute were sent to the Court of Justice of the European Community, the national diplomatic missions to the Community, the United Nations Economic Commission for Europe, the International Labor Organization, the European Payments Union, the party organizations of the member nations, and the Economic and Social Councils of member governments. In all, five thousand copies were disseminated.[9] Among the institutions of the Community, the statute got its strongest support from the European Parliament, which urged action on the ECSC executive in the strongest possible terms.

Although the trade union organization's secretariat and committees are constantly stating positions to the Common Market on various issues before the Community, the organization attempts to make an impact on the labor movement and the public at large by means of periodic congresses in Brussels. A large press corps is attracted to these gatherings, where the highest Community officers and the most highly placed Socialist politicians are heard in plenary sessions. About a half-dozen general policy issues are raised for debate in working sessions at which the hundreds of delegates are apprised of the state of the organization's thinking on issues and have an opportunity to exchange views. The Community personalities that address the assemblies are not apt to stay for the discussions, but any declarations adopted by the assembly are communicated to them and hopefully will make the front pages of the newspapers.

The Common Market Commission encourages the activity of pressure groups in Brussels and for good reasons. Since it is the sectors of European life represented by these groups that the Common Market will be serving or regulating, effective lines of communication have to be developed with them so that policies can be formed in the context of all relevant facts and interests. And the Commission wants to promote European thinking among national interest groups by creating associations at the Common Market

[9] L'Intersyndicale C.E.C.A., *Rapport d'activité*, Luxembourg, 11 decembre 1961, p. 8 [mimeographed].

level. The pressure groups can assist the Commission too by lobbying for its policies in national capitals. A special affinity between
the Brussels lobbies and the European Commission results from
the fact that many groups, besides pursuing their own interests
within the framework of the Common Market, are dedicated to
European integration and provide free publicity on its behalf.

Some national groups, lobbying at home capitals on their own
behalf, take strong interest in the work of the Community, too,
such as the French National Council of Employers, which has
followed Community activities meticulously from the time the
Rome Treaty was negotiated. One of their leaders was named by
the French government to one of its two seats in the Commission
in 1958.

Public Without Opinion

Europe is above all a state of mind, and the degree to which
Europe can function as an entity depends on the extent to which
it is *regarded* as an entity. But the activity of the Common Market
in Brussels is not the object of general public attention and interest.
Europeans are, in general, indifferent to the Common Market, a
situation due to ignorance about the institution. Much public relations work, whether by private associations, public agencies, or
individual businessmen or educators, aims to impress upon the
European public the simple fact that the Common Market exists.
If there were to be a popular election of deputies to the European
Parliament in the near future, the electorate could be expected to
be indifferent to it, not knowing what they were being asked to
vote for.

There has been a more intense public reaction to the Common
Market in the United States than there has been in Europe. Americans saw the European Community at once as a new economic
threat, as a new source of Western strength in the Cold War, and
as an opportunity for expanding American trade. In any case the
Common Market was an important new *external* force, for good
or ill, and it caught the average American a little off balance and
made him alert.

In Europe, on the other hand, the Common Market symbolizes something entirely different. The coincidence of the Common Market and the recent growth in European earnings has generated some incipient enthusiasm for the institution, but enthusiasm is not knowledge or understanding. Europeans are apt to visualize the Common Market as a means for greater European industrial and world power, which would make Europe more independent of the United States and of greater concern to the Soviet Union; and such thoughts produce in a European a new sense of self-respect that make him willing to defend the actions of the Common Market, right or wrong. Loyalty, however, is not knowledge either. To the Common Market, enthusiasm and loyalty are assests worth cultivating broadly, and so it encourages publicity of an undifferentiated sort, such as "Common Market" sales at big department stores, "Common Market" exhibitions at fairs and "United States of Europe" posters aimed at simply keeping the idea of Europe before the public like the name of a political candidate or of a commercial product. But such shallow popularity is scattered, intermittent, and fickle.

The European press does not take the initiative in orienting the European mind to the Common Market. Common Market news *is* news, but it has to give up space on the front pages of the newspapers to local disasters, to news of national importance, to news of Southeast Asian, African, or other crises, and even to news of the United Nations, an institution generally more remote to the average European than the Common Market. Remote though the United Nations might be, its actions in the Congo, in Cyprus, or in Cambodia or its discussions of disarmament, apartheid, or the representation of Red China are all more newsworthy than some new Common Market regulation on the tobacco tariff. A citizen of Brussels might take pride in the fact that the Common Market is located there and be grateful for the boost it gives to the commerce of the city. Also, he might have hated the United Nations for, in his eyes, having preempted Belgian rights in the Congo. Of these two, his feeling about the United Nations is the more intense, and he would have been eager for the least scrap of Congo news on the front page. News of the North Atlantic Treaty Organization takes precedence over Common Market news for similar reasons.

In short, from day to day the front page of a European newspaper looks much the same as it did before the Common Market began.

Study of the United Nations played an important part in higher education in Europe after the end of the war, but the academic community moved very slowly in extending its interests to the Common Market, with the notable exception of the small College of Europe in Bruges, Belgium, which is dedicated to European studies. Common Market studies found their way into the curricula of the larger universities only after a half decade, but the mid-1960's saw a rush to make up for lost time as full-blown institutes for European studies were being started by the universities of Paris (1963), for instance, and Brussels (1964). Courses offered in 1965-66 represented a fifty per cent increase over those offered in 1964-65 (see Table 1). Most universities in France and the Low Coun-

Table 1 [1]

COURSES AND SEMINARS CONCERNING EUROPEAN INTEGRATION AT EUROPEAN UNIVERSITIES [2]

	School Year 1964-65	School Year 1965-66
France	59	69
Germany	32	40
Great Britain	11	32
Belgium	17	26
Italy	10	21
Switzerland	12	17
The Netherlands	4	10

[1] From *Communauté européenne*, 10° année, No. 9, septembre, 1966, p. 11.
[2] Excluding institutions not under the national educational systems.

tries introduced courses on European integration, and Italy attempted to start a European university. German universities have programs, too, but they trail behind France. Not only do German universities lack departments of political science, but German intellectuals are ambivalent about the Common Market. They include the type of Social Democrat who has misgivings about jeopardizing German reunification by too close a link with a West European capitalist customs union. All universities in the Six have to struggle against conservative law professors who either resist giving a place to studies of the Community or threaten to restrict study to the juridical aspects of the Community.

In Europe, more than in the United States, public opinion lags behind the initiative of the educated elite, and the elite is therefore freer to take important initial action toward the achievement of European unity without rigid adherence to public opinion. It was just such initiative that created the Common Market in the first place. Public opinion statistics were often alarming and frustrating.

How did European peoples regard each other? Professional opinion-research agencies operating in several European countries prepared data under the aegis of the United Nations Educational Scientific and Cultural Organization during the latter 1940's, using matched questionnaires and matched samples of over one thousand persons in each country. In the report prepared by William Buchanan and Hadley Cantril,[10] France, Germany, Italy, and the Netherlands showed more friendliness toward the United States than toward any of their fellow members of the Six, markedly so in the cases of Germany and the Netherlands and especially Italy. To the French, three other countries were on a par with the United States, but only one of these, Belgium, was a member of the Six. Speaking only of the Six, Italians showed a significant degree of friendliness toward France and to a lesser extent, Germany; and in the Netherlands, Belgium was high in esteem, with France following considerably behind. Germany showed no particular friendliness toward any of the Six, but showed some preference for the Dutch.

The emergence of the Cold War in the mid-1940's placed the Soviet Union at the head of the list of nations toward which unfriendliness was shown in Germany, Italy, and the Netherlands, but the French were still unfriendliest toward Germany, with the Soviet Union a close second. The only other marked unfriendliness existing among the Six was French dislike for Italians and an unfriendliness of Germans toward the French.

In short, the Six were lukewarm or worse toward one another,

[10] *How Nations See Each Other, A Study in Public Opinion.* Urbana, Ill.: University of Illinois Press, 1953, Chap. 7 and Appendix D.

feeling greater kinship elsewhere—with the United States, for example, or with Britain or Sweden. And so the European institutions beginning in the late 1940's were more like marriages of convenience than love matches. One could not expect fondness among peoples whose organizing principles had been separation and nationalism for so long. Moreover, there was a basic dislike for Germany among neighboring countries, which made the Community appear to be a kind of sacrifice calculated to guarantee an end to quarrels across the Rhine.

Unfriendliness toward Germany may have become anachronistic, but it is nevertheless still there. With each passing year, Germany's neighbors have found new ways to nurse their grudges. They have envied the rapid industrial advance of Germany; they have condemned the behavior of German tourists; they have cultivated snobbism against German culture. The day has yet to dawn when a German can travel abroad in countries of the Six without doors being closed to him on account of his nationality, without people whispering behind his back, or without being mistreated in areas where there was greatest devastation during the wars. One effort to counteract international prejudice is the private European Foundation for International Exchanges, which arranges for thousands of ordinary citizens and their families to trade jobs and houses temporarily so as to gain an appreciation of life across the Rhine or elsewhere.[11] The keystone, the hope of European unity, still remains that enunciated by Robert Schuman on May 9, 1950, "The gathering together of the European nations requires that the age-old opposition between France and Germany be eliminated: the action undertaken should in the first place affect France and Germany." [12]

Mutual dislikes are normally far back in a European's mind, fortunately, where they are thrust by the parochialism of everyday life. A Frenchman normally sees only Frenchmen from his own region and thoughts of closer dealings with other nationalities do

[11] From the paper by Foundation director Lucien Radoux, presented to the United States National Commission for UNESCO Conference, Chicago, Oct. 24, 1963 [mimeographed].

[12] This speech proclaiming the Schuman Plan has assumed a place comparable to the American Declaration of Independence in European patriotic literature, and May 9 has become Europe's "national day."

not ordinarily enter his mind. The idea of integration, in other words, is extraneous to the average man. Hopes for the unity of Europe remain in the realm of theory, and he can afford to be idealistic about them. He is also the dormant gull of nationalist demagogues.

During 1962 four European opinion-research organizations collaborated on the first extensive and coordinated survey of opinion on the Common Market and European unity. The results[13] (see Table 2) showed that the citizens of the European Community were over-

Table 2

ARE YOU FOR OR AGAINST THE EFFORTS
FOR EUROPEAN UNIFICATION?

	In per cent		
	For	Against	No Answer
Belgium	65	5	30
France	72	8	20
Germany	81	4	15
Italy	60	4	36
Luxembourg	27	5	68
The Netherlands	87	4	9

whelmingly in favor of the unification of Europe, with usually only about four or five per cent being opposed. The survey also showed a favorable increase over earlier postwar figures. Whereas a 1952 survey in Germany had found about three-quarters of the respondents favorable to unity, the 1962 survey found four-fifths favorable. In France, too, a 1947 survey found two-thirds in favor, while the 1962 survey found three-quarters in favor. Although the European elite were the driving force behind integration, they were by no means alone in favoring unity.

Optimism about an early achievement of unity was generally strong, with Germans, French, Italians, and Belgians gauging that unity would be achieved within the next ten years (see Table 3). Only a tenth or less of the respondents in Belgium, France, Italy,

[13] Data here is quoted from *Communauté européenne,* 6ᵉ année, No. 12, decembre 1962, pp. 9-12.

Table 3

WHEN WILL EUROPE UNITE?

In per cent

	Belgium	France	Germany	Italy	Luxem-bourg	The Neth-erlands
Never	9	11	17	9	6	18
In several generations	9	12	4	3	10	11
In 20 to 30 years	14	14	10	8	18	23
In 10 to 15 years	20	14	16	9	12	21
In the next 10 years	23	21	26	10	14	15
No answer	25	28	27	61	20	12
Total	100	100	100	100	100	100

and Luxembourg thought that unity would never be achieved. And, although seventeen and eighteen per cent respectively in Germany and the Netherlands thought unity would never come, these were the two peoples most eager for unity and therefore the most sensitive to discouragement.

Respondents were most apt to construe unity in political terms. A quarter of them considered unity a guarantee against the kind of quarrels that had reduced Europe to rubble twice during the twentieth century. A second category of respondents (one-sixth) cited the weakness of separate European states as a reason for unity. Greater ability to contain the Soviet bloc was mentioned third by one-seventh of the respondents. Only one-tenth saw the possible emergence of Europe as a third Super Power to be a value of unity, a reaction that harmonized well with the antiwar sentiment also expressed by the largest group of respondents.

About one-sixth of the respondents in France and Germany could see benefits to their economies resulting from unity. Most respondents thought in terms of improving *over-all* economies, but the Italians saw rises in their personal incomes as a possible benefit of unity. In general the economic interests of the respondents appeared somewhat theoretical and impersonal, a vague hope in which personal gain was only dimly seen.

The idea that there might be any cultural or moral gain in unity was expressed by only a few respondents in France and the

Netherlands, where it was the third-ranking response after the political and economic responses.

Although most respondents knew little about the Common Market and valued chiefly the political benefits of unity, they liked the specific economic measures of the Community when told what they were (see Table 4). There was overwhelming approval of Common

Table 4

ARE YOU FOR OR AGAINST THE FOLLOWING MEASURES?

	Average percentage for all six countries, weighted according to size of country	
	For	*Against*
Elimination of tariffs in Europe	81	6
Free circulation of workers in Europe	68	16
Equating of diplomas given by schools in Europe	72	4
A common foreign policy for Europe	60	9
Common administration of scientific research in Europe	75	3
A common farm policy	69	8
Common standards of social welfare throughout Europe	77	4
Subsidizing development of poor areas of Europe	49	28
Subsidizing African development	35	40

Market measures to liberalize European trade, to internationalize institutions of higher learning, to formulate a common foreign policy, to pool scientific research, to unify agricultural policy, and to harmonize European social security systems. There was a significant amount of fear (sixteen per cent against) of the free movement of labor in Europe. But this was a natural fear, and a large majority (sixty-eight per cent) were in favor of free movement. Respondents divided over Common Market programs for aid to poor European regions and underdeveloped African nations, but such a division would exist even if Europe were united; it exists in the United States over the question of foreign aid.

Responses varied according to the class of the respondents. In-dustrialists and professionals were the most favorable to European union, while the farmers were the most reticent. Although a major-ity of the farmers favored a common agricultural market, it was only a bare majority in Germany and in several other countries there was strong opposition. In Italy, there was widespread in-difference. A large number of negative respondents were willing to admit that although they expected agriculture to suffer from the Common Market now, they could see it benefiting in the long run, all except the German farmers, who were thoroughgoing pessimists.

Small-businessmen were generally ignorant of the Common Mar-ket and feared the implications of change for their shops. When informed of some specific Common Market step such as the eliminat-ing of trade barriers, however, they were overwhelmingly in favor. Laborers were in large part indifferent to European unity and pol-icy; but, when told of specific steps that would affect them directly, there were likewise few opposed.

Women among the respondents were less well informed than the men and hesitated to take part in the survey. The Common Market figured least in the thinking of youths, who had grown up in a Europe that was in the process of unifying and who took it for granted.

Repeated surveys using the same respondents might have been valuable in the years following 1962, but the Gaullist French government refused to allow the Community to repeat the survey. Possibly the evidence of popular support for European unity was an embarrassment. Nonetheless a few smaller surveys were made by private polling institutes in Germany and France.[14] The German public, already shown to be unusually pessimistic about the pros-pect for unity in 1962, grew increasingly pessimistic, with the percentage of those who anticipated eventual European unity dropping from thirty-six per cent in 1961 to twenty-nine per cent in 1965. The Germans tended to see progress in the work for in-tegration, however. In February, 1966, French opinion was found to be more concerned about the Common Market than any other

[14] L'Opinion publique et l'Europe, *Communauté européenne*. Paris, 10ᵉ année, No. 5, mai 1966, p. 3.

outstanding problem the respondents could mention, and approval of French participation in a European union with centralized powers showed an increase from thirty-eight per cent in 1962 to fifty-five per cent in 1966.[15]

The main responsibility for molding public opinion falls on the shoulders of the Community, which has a central information service as well as press relations offices attached to each of the principal institutions. The Press and Information Service alone spent about $3,800,000 during 1966, an amount approaching that spent by the Department of Public Information of the United Nations. Various other Community institutions invest in informational activities, such as press bureaus, internships, and university scholarships, which makes the actual total expenditure a great deal larger. The work of the Community is reinforced, moreover, by the information disseminated by the European Movement, by Common Market lobbies, by schools, and by private individuals and firms.

Information programs in Europe operate under certain handicaps. There is a European tradition of secrecy in government. And past European governments, especially during the Nazi era, exploited information media for sinister purposes, which cast suspicion on the very nature of governmental information programs. Also, language differences between the Common Market publics is a perpetual drag on information work.

The most important medium at the disposal of the Community is the press. By 1966 there were over a hundred reporters accredited to the Commission and almost a thousand recipients of press releases. At first the Community was ill prepared to meet the press, and the European newspapers were short of personnel versed in the Community institutions or policy problems under discussion. Information provided reporters by the Community had certain inadequacies, such as failing to take into account its novice readership; and until 1964 there were no background papers to explain the significance of press releases. Even a cryptic press release on what resulted from a meeting (all meetings were closed to the press except plenary meetings of the Parliament) was often too brief for

---

[15] The percentage favoring a union with centralized powers was bound to be lower than the percentage favoring efforts to unify Europe in some unspecified way.

an informed correspondent to grasp what had happened. Press conferences for Community figures were an inadequate substitute, because the reporters did not know what to ask. Correspondents insisted on referring to regulations passed by the Council of Ministers as "agreements"—as much as to say they were treaties settling some matter once and for all rather than legislative steps in a continual process of development. Newspaper articles appeared in America saying only that "something" was up in Brussels; and, when more than one meeting of the Council of Ministers was necessary to finish a debate, it was reported as a "deadlock" threatening to destroy the Common Market. Experience among the Common Market press corps eventually solved some problems. And in 1965 the press corps accredited to the Commission formed an association to improve its work and opportunities.

What about information that was not news? Many of the internal documents of the Community are of interest to outsiders, and these are printed and sold or given away. They include such documents as the records of the European Parliament, the annual reports of the excutives, the *Official Journal* of the Community, statistical reports, and monthly bulletins. They are distributed centrally from Brussels and Luxembourg and also from branch offices in each of the other capitals of the Community and in key capitals abroad. Although slow in doing so, the Brussels executives took some steps to establish depository libraries both within the Community and abroad. The governing institution of the Common Market, the Council of Ministers, publishes no documents at all from its own household, and its only public record is its body of decisions appearing in the *Official Journal* published by the Commission.

The popularization of Community information in the form of exerpts from speeches, colorful pamphlet surveys of Community activities, and simplified monthly reviews of Community affairs is carried on by highly sophisticated techniques; and the formats used are the least restrained of any comparable publications by European governments or international organizations. Moreover, there is no public communication medium that is overlooked—radio, television, exhibitions at fairs, traveling exhibits, film strips, sound recordings, sponsorship of seminars and conferences, and the conduct of tours and lectures at headquarters. The development of electronic media is only beginning, but it is focused where it can do the most good, such as on West African associated nations where the dissemination of literature is difficult.

The Community is trying to penetrate specific centers of ignorance and potential hostility to the unification of Europe, and the professional opinion survey of 1962 was sponsored by the Community expressly for the purpose of singling out groups on which special attention should be concentrated. The most important targets turned out to be farmers, industrial workers, and women.

Commissioner Lemaignen suspected that the governments were fearful of Community autonomy in information,[16] and the community is not entirely free to use media of its choice on the target of its choice. Not only did the Gaullist government frown on expansion of the staff of the Community's information office in Paris and threaten to remonstrate if the publications of that office were critical of official French action, it also restricted the Commission in Brussels. The Commission had been in the practice of publishing its proposals to the Council as supplements to the monthly EEC *Bulletin,* but the French demanded an end to the practice of publication prior to Council action as one of the conditions for their returning to Brussels after their boycott.

The Common Market will eventually get a lot of publicity as a by-product of the economic regulations that are beginning to touch the lives of Europeans, and Europeans will accustom themselves to regulation by the Community. The sense and appearance of oneness that is resulting from the freedom of movement achieved by the Community is having a more profound effect on public opinion than any number of information programs. Women's fashions and the format of women's magazines is already "unified," for instance, as is the European taste in toys. Europe may begin to look like a nation before it becomes one, and that appearance can have a unifying effect in itself.

[16] Robert Lemaignen, *L'Europe au Berceau.* Paris: Plom, 1964, p. 64.

The Court

VII

The seven-member Court of Justice of the European Community was first housed in the Villa Vauban in Luxembourg City not far from the buildings of the European Coal and Steel Community. This city, cleft by landscaped and fortress-flanked gorges, was the home of the Schuman Plan organization after 1952, as it had been at one time the home of Robert Schuman himself. The Court soon outgrew the Villa, as the staff expanded to handle an ever-increasing volume of litigation; and it entered quarters in a new, glass-fronted building on one of Luxembourg's main streets. It was to be left behind in Luxembourg when the CSC moved to Brussels. When in 1958 the Court took jurisdiction over the new Euratom and Common Market communities, it was already a going concern with a backlog of cases on its docket and with a fairly clear understanding of its role and potentialities.

The lineage of the Court looks different from different points of view. The maintenance of legal checks on administration has always been more highly developed in continental Europe than in the Anglo-American legal world, and in such countries as France and Italy it takes the form of an administrative court system. When setting up the Schuman Plan agency, it was routine to include a checking mechanism, the Court of Justice. The court has always remained within its administrative role, and there has never been any effort to broaden its jurisdiction to torts and crimes, which make up the vast majority of ordinary court cases. From the point of view of the three communities, however, the Court of Justice acts as a supreme court for them, and their goal is to evolve it into the supreme court of a federal European union. Here the inspiration has been the Supreme Court of the United States, which had an influence on European constitution writing after the Second World War when France created its Constitutional Committee, West Germany its Constitutional Court, and Italy its Constitutional Court.

Leap of Faith

The Court has a power that has no peer in Europe, to enforce the treaties over any conflicting laws, rules or administrative acts of the member nations. In the treaties six nations undertook certain promises to one another, and it was up to each one to fulfill the promises by setting its own legal household in order. But the Rome Treaty was a new kind of treaty. It created a law-*making* Community whose subsequent enactments would all have the same superiority over national laws as the Treaty itself, because they were extensions of the Treaty. The Schuman Plan had served as a pilot project for this kind of treaty, but in 1958 the Rome Treaty placed the whole European economy under the Community's jurisdiction.

The advocates and supporters of the Community made a leap of faith. To promote European unity they temporarily abandoned the democratic patterns and the supremacy of law that were the foundation of Western government. Not a single Common Market official is elected to his post by the people. Not a single Common Market regulation is enacted by a parliament, not even by the Community's own Parliament. National laws no longer have certainty because national legislation contrary to Community law can be held inapplicable.

The grand design was that with a tolerable delay the European Parliament *would* be popularly elected and *would* have the last word over Community legislation, and until that time the abandonment of Western traditions could be overlooked. It fell to the lot of the European Court to rationalize the legitimacy of Community law, and there was much in its favor. The whole apparatus of the Community glorified the passage of European regulations that would advance the cause of unity. Even the Parliament, which was most abused by the order within the Community, made a special effort to promote respect for Community law by national authorities.[1]

A statesman who is *unwilling* to make the leap of faith can make a strong case against the validity of Community regulations. In the political realm, President de Gaulle pointed out at the time of the French boycott that the Community lacked the democratic paraphernalia to legitimize its enactments. In the judicial realm, the Financial Court of Rhineland-Palatinate advised that the German government could not confer the lawmaking power of the Diet on *any* other institution, the Common Market included, and, if it did, it would lay the way open for the very kind of arbitrary use of power that the whole struggle for legal government in Germany was directed against.[2] If one could give arbitrary powers to the Common Market today, one could give them to a neo-Hitler tomorrow, or the Common Market could. A committee of the European Parliament in commenting on the Rhineland-Palatinate opinion said that the problem of dictatorship did not arise in transferring powers to the European Community because the Community recognized "fundamental and human rights and are ready to protect the freedom of the individual, the family, and property." [3] The committee was stretching a point, however, because nowhere in the Rome Treaty were there any express guarantees of civil rights. The committee noted how European governments had precedent for conferring limited rule-making power on regulatory bodies, but it was difficult to see what was *limited* about the powers of the Common Market. Is the power to fix the price of food a limited power?

The enthusiasm for European integration has swept along most of the European judicial profession, which was satisfied to apply the law as written in the treaties and regulations of the Community. The European court above all has the responsibility to be blind to arguments against the validity of Community lawmaking.

[1] European Parliament, Legal Committee, Report . . . on the Paramountcy of Community Law over the Laws of Member States, *Working Documents*, No. 43, May 25, 1965.

[2] Quoted in *Ibid.*, pp. 15-17. In 1965 the opinion was being referred to the German Constitutional Court.

[3] *Ibid.*, p. 18.

On December 1, 1965, the gauntlet was thrown down, and on a complaint from the European Commission the Court invalidated (*Commission v. the Italian Republic*) an Italian system of rebates to manufacturers that violated the Treaty. The rebates were based *not* upon administrative action of the kind that had been corrected by the Court in previous actions, but upon Italian law! If the law passed by the Italian parliament, the voice of the Italian people, were not trimmed in so far as it conflicted with the Treaty of Rome, to that degree the Rome Treaty would have been a dead letter. That was the logic of Community law, and such confrontations were unavoidable. The Court protested repeatedly that it had no power to deal with internal legislation, it could only annul official actions based on the legislation that were contrary to the Treaty— a neat fiction.

Professors as Judges

There is a great deal of prestige in membership in the Court of Justice—not quite as much prestige as in the International Court of Justice at The Hague, and the salaries are lower, but the Court in Luxembourg has the more desirable work of the two. It has, above all, more work; it rendered thirty-eight decisions during 1965. Election to the Court has been the apex of the careers of its members, and for the most part its judges were appointed in their fifties. One term of six years might take a judge to retirement age, and two terms were very likely to do so although there is no rule compelling retirement. Since the Court was created in connection with the Coal and Steel Community in 1952, some of its veteran judges had already retired in their late sixties and seventies by 1966, and one judge of 68 and one of 71 still retained their seats at that time. The end-of-career aspect of the judgeships is as near as the European Community has came to approximating the life tenure characteristic of ordinary judgeships in Europe. One drawback to service on the Court is that, if a judge's tenure should end after the first six years while he is in his fifties, the return to favorable employment at home could be difficult. One Dutchman whose term was not renewed was appointed to an appeals bench in his homeland, but one Italian simply went into private law practice.

Fixing the term at six years did not give governments political influence over individual judges. They cannot pressure a judge by threatening not to nominate him for another term. All opinions of the court are joint opinions, and there are no dissenting opinions. The views and votes of an individual judge can be and *are* kept the deepest of all Court secrets. A government has no way of knowing whether its national on the bench has been "loyal."

The organization of the Court is patterned after the administrative court of France, the Council of State. The seven judges of the European Court are political appointees, like those of the Council of State, and they are assisted in their work by two advocates general who prepare the briefs, like the Council of State's government commissioners. One of the first advocates general *was* a French government commissioner. These nine offices together with that of Registrar, which heads the secretariat of the Court, have been distributed among the six member governments as equitably as possible, with at least one judgeship and usually one other office going to each of the six member countries. The countries that have to content themselves with only one of these ten offices are Luxembourg and the country whose national is president of the Court at any given time. Geographical distribution of judges is just as valuable to the Court as it is to any of the other Community institutions in that it keeps the Court in touch with local law and practice throughout the Community, but there is one irritation. The simultaneous interpreters that are so much a part of European Community institutions are not admitted into any secret deliberations of the Court, and so some judges who are not fluent in French, the language of such meetings, are limited in their degree of participation. In public hearings interpretation is available in any Community language, however.

Although the judges of the court have nearly all had legal training, they have not necessarily followed judicial careers. The majority of the Court have been law professors, and about half the Court have been judges before; in some cases for very brief periods. A few attained prominence in ministries of justice, and one had been the French Minister of Justice. One was the *brother* of a minister of justice,[4] and a few had been politicians, that is to say parliamentarians.

The fact that there are political factors bearing on the composition of the Court does not distinguish it greatly from the highest courts of the member governments, and the Court probably benefits from having judges who have not spent their careers on the bench. The technical character and political overtones of the cases dealt with by the court required the judges to be alert to the politics, administration, and economics of their respective countries—much more so than to the purely legal norms relating to taxes, damages, and family life that are the main concern of an ordinary judge.

About half of the court is renewed every three years, four judge-ships one time and three the next. The specific choice of a candidate rests entirely in the hands of each nation's council of ministers, especially the foreign minister. The Treaty provided that judges be chosen "by agreement among the member governments,"[5] but, when one of a government's quota of offices is vacated, that government is fairly sure of seating whomever it chooses. Some representative of the Six could theoretically block agreement, but the fear of retaliation against a candidate from his own government discourages that. The Court can remove its own members if it finds them unable to do their jobs, and a judge in question cannot vote on his own case.[6]

From Pillar to Post

The Court of Justice emerged in 1952 with extraordinary powers, considering that it was an international court. Not only could it hear cases of private firms, going over the heads of their governments, but also it could test the constitutionality (i.e., fidelity to the Schuman Plan Treaty) of actions of the political organs of the

---

[4] Reported in *Nieue Rotterdamse Courant*, Oct. 12, 1961, and *France Industrielle*, Dec. 26, 1961, according to Werner Field, The Judges of the Court of Justice of the European Communities, *Villanova Law Review*, IX, 1963-1964: 45.

[5] Communauté économique européenne, *Traité instituant la Communauté économique européenne et documents annexes.* Bruxelles, 1957, Art. 167.

[6] *Ibid.*, Statute de la Cour de justice, Art. 6.

Schuman Plan, punish noncompliance with coal and steel regulations by means of fines and other sanctions, and participate in the amendment of the Schuman Plan Treaty. No international court had ever had so much power before.

Enforcing the regulations of the Schuman Plan was similar to the kind of work done by the ordinary national courts in Europe, and such work engrossed the Court more than any other aspect of its work. For instance, the Court had dozens of cases that arose from enforcement of a temporary price control regulation for scrap iron that was terminated in 1959, and the cases dragged on for years afterward. Under the regulation a company's own scrap iron was exempt from the price control; and, although there was no question of the constitutionality of the regulation, the court had to decide cases from individual steel firms testing whether this or that kind of corporate relationship would allow a company to call scrap iron its own. (Was scrap owned by a subsidiary one's own?)

But those were the first days. The Rome Treaty added immeasurably to the responsibilities of the Court by assigning it the Common Market's cases. By the end of 1961, the Court had not yet decided any Common Market cases, and its seventy decisions over the previous nine years all dealt with the Schuman Plan. By the end of 1965 the Court had decided seventy-six Common Market cases, and the rate of increase of such cases promised to press ECSC cases to the periphery very quickly. The number of Common Market cases decided by the Court would have been much greater had not the Rome Treaty given jurisdiction to national courts over cases involving application of Common Market regulations to private parties. Those courts had decided 103 such cases by the end of 1965, more cases than the European Court.[7]

The principle of the Rome Treaty[8] was that, if problems of interpretation of Community law could be referred to the European Court for its advice, the Court could maintain consistency in the application of the law among the Six.[9] And, in fact, in deciding

---

[7] A tabulation of cases as of Dec. 31, 1965, is in Commission, *Neuvième rapport général,* pp. 421, 436-437.

[8] Art. 177.

[9] Michael Gaudet, head of the Community's legal section, explained this philosophy in *Annales de droit et de sciences politique.* Bruxelles, Tome XXI, No. 2, 1961.

their 103 cases the national courts requested interpretive opinions from the European Court 20 times. For example, a private suit was brought against a member of the European Parliament in a national court, which asked the European Court in turn whether the member was immune from legal process under the Community's Protocol on Privileges and Immunities. The question arose from the fact that the protocol extended immunity during the sessions of the Parliament, but the Parliament held only one year-long session with one-week sittings monthly and a suspension of the session in between. The answer of the European Court (*Wagner v. Fohrmann and Krier*, 1964) was that the session lasted up to adjournment at the end of the year, through sittings and suspensions alike. Without the advice of the European Court, the national court might have decided the other way, that the immunity of parliamentarians was meant to keep them free of interference only at sittings and going to and from sittings.

To assume that this form of consultation would unify European law might have been wishful thinking, however. There were two faults in the system: (1) Requests by national courts for interpretations by the European Court were *voluntary*, and (2) if the interpretation was wrongly applied by the national court after it had been handed down, there was nothing the European Court could do about it; there was no provision for appeal.[10] Already by 1966 some small danger signs were appearing. There were four different national practices, for example, regarding the clause[11] of the antitrust regulation that reserved competence over antitrust cases to national courts if the European Commission had not taken action on them: (1) A French Court regarded the Commission as having exclusive jurisdiction; (2) on the basis of general principles of law, not on the basis of Common Market law, a Belgian court decided to suspend judgment until the Commission had acted; (3) a German court acted immediately and held that the antitrust regulations had not been violated unless the Commission had said they had;

[10] As pointed out by Robert Lecourt, former French Minister of Justice and member of the Court, in Community's Court of Justice Builds Community Law, *European Community*. Washington: No. 65, Sept., 1963, p. 13.

[11] Regulation No. 17, Art. 9, Para. 3, *Journal officiel*, 5ᵉ année, No. 13, 21 fevrier 1962, p. 207.

and (4) another French court suspended its action. This was not equal justice, and the situation was likely to get worse.[12]

In order to make the most of the voluntary system for consultation between the European Court and national courts, the European Court tried its best to be friendly. In its opinion on a case in 1966, the European Court said it wanted to *cooperate* with the National courts and would not stand on ceremony with them (*le refus de toute rigueur formaliste*).[13] But that was not law; that was public relations. The legal service of the Community executive is able to help in the unification of legal practice in the Community by coping with the huge demand for information about Community law addressed to the Community by lawyers, judges, and universities. And over an extended period possibly a strong educational program by the Community can be as effective in maintaining European legal standards as the opinions of the European Court on questions posed by national courts. Both education and cooperation are makeshift, nonetheless. They can never fully substitute for a grant of power to the European Court to *order* up questions from national courts that *it* thinks it should settle and the power to hear *appeals* from judgments by national courts.

Baring the Teeth

The word of the Court *is* law, direct and final, in suits by Community institutions, by governments, or by individuals challenging Community action or inaction. It can also invalidate the actions of national officials on petition from the Commission, and it is the arbiter in complaints of the Community's personnel over their contracts. In such actions the teeth of the Rome Treaty are bared. That the court would be cautious in exercising its power to interpret the Treaty was indicated in 1962, when in answer to the first preliminary question posed it under the Common Market Treaty it decided that the antitrust articles of the Treaty could not be applied without some specific implementing regulations passed by Community institutions (*De Geus v. Bosch et al*). The Court did

[12] Commission, *Neuvième rapport général*, p. 435.
[13] *Ibid.*, p. 426.

not wish to prejudice the eventual administration of the antitrust provisions by trying a little lawmaking of its own, even though the basic antitrust rules had been laid down in the Rome Treaty and had been in force since 1958.

In the first contentious case of the Common Market (1961), the Court found the Italian government at fault and upheld the Commission's charge that an Italian tax on pork imports from the Community was illegal. And for a period, after a few more cases, it looked as if the Commission could not lose in its contests with member governments. Finally on July 4, 1963, the Court rejected the Commission's grounds for reducing a German import quota for wine and granted the German government's petition for annulment of the Commission's action. The third side of the triangle of contestants, wronged citizens, first gained satisfaction through the Court under the Rome Treaty when on July 1, 1965, some German importers obtained an annulment of a Commission decision allowing the German government to apply safeguards against the importation of corn (*Töpfer v. Commission*). Here both the Commission and the German government were found wrong at once, the government for requesting application of the safeguard and the Commission for granting it.

Although the Court has proved to be an effective remedy for some types of wrongs, there is a loophole. In its annual report of 1966, the Commission complained of the problem of "successive infractions" of the Treaty.[14] Governments might take temporary measures, ostensibly under safeguard provisions of the Treaty, and maintain a de facto situation permanently in violation of the Treaty, relenting from time to time after intervention by the Commission or the Court. The Court has no equity or tort powers, and it can be given the run around.

The one subject over which the Court's jurisdiction is airtight is the settlement of complaints by Eurocrats over their contracts. This work is unpleasant. With the personnel regulations for the Common Market and Euratom coming into force in 1962, the Court had as many cases of civil servants contesting their failure to receive tenure as it had cases of any other type. Normally Euratom cases are personnel cases. Although most of the grudges were soon

[14] Commission, *Neuvième rapport général*, p. 429.

quieted, the life of the Court was for years as much that of a grievance committee as a high arbiter of international conflicts. When the Court did find that an employee had been wronged, it was especially liberal with compensation. In *Lachmueller v. E.E.C. Commission* (1960) the Court recognized the right of the Commission to let Lachmueller go but granted him $12,000 because it considered him wronged by the way his case was handled. To those who were disappointed when permanent appointments were confirmed, the Court normally had to say no and share the burden of conscience with the Commission.

Despite the loopholes in the Court's supervision of national courts and its difficulty in dealing with successive violations, it is nevertheless the Court that wields the Community's sword, and it has come under its share of criticism. The German Ruhr coal operators carried on a running battle with the Coal and Steel Community over the legality of creating a unified sales organization for Ruhr coal, for instance. The ECSC forced a number of reorganizations, but there was a tendency on the part of the Ruhr firms to backslide toward their sales pool. Finally in 1962 (*Ruhrkohlen-Verkaufsgesellschaften v. High Authority*) the Court outlawed the pool and decided at least three sales organizations would have to exist in order to meet the antitrust standards of the Schuman Plan Treaty, but there was nothing it could say in its opinion that would make the Ruhr coal operators believe it had been economically right. They criticized the opinion and went on fighting it. In connection with the scrap iron cases the Court had come under fire from popular periodicals such as *der Spiegel* in Germany and from the public relations facilities of the Mannesmann firm, whose interests had suffered in connection with the Court's definition of an *enterprise*.[15]

Possibly there is a remedy for criticism of the Court. Professor Werner Feld, echoing similar suggestions by judges of the Court, expressed concern over the fact that the Community provided no mechanism for appeal of the Court's judgments.[16] Quite apart from

---

[15] Criticisms documented in Werner Feld, *The Court of the European Communities, New Dimension in International Adjudication*. The Hague: Martinus Nijhoff, 1964, pp. 74-78.

[16] *Ibid.*, pp. 74-122.

the intelligence and good will of the judges of the Court, it is perhaps true that citizens of Western nations have habituated themselves to the notion that there is always the *possibility* of at least one appeal from a judgment in any just system of government. When the volume of European litigation comes to warrant the employment of more judges[17] and more courts, the creation of even a simple hierarchy might do a lot to build respect for decisions of the Court.

Still, in its primitive years, the Court was winning its battle. None of its decisions have been flouted; but that is good fortune, not necessity. It is not possible to assume that, if a government refused to end a practice contrary to the Treaty, on Court order, it would be read out of the Common Market. It is very possible that, if a choice lay between flouting a court decision and dissolving the Common Market, some sort of face-saving and Community-saving compromise would be sought. It would have been just as possible for the French boycott to have been caused by some decision of the Court as by a recommendation of the Commission. Court decisions are as firm as the Community itself—no more and no less.

[17] The Council can create additional judgeships.

Neighbors

VIII

International operations of a nondiplomatic character—lend lease, foreign aid, educational exchanges, and the like—have given the world the *shirt-sleeve* diplomat. The Common Market has introduced the *business-suit* diplomat. The De Gaulle government has objected to the Commission's practice of dressing formally to receive foreign ambassadors. By June, 1966, seventy-four countries from all over the free world were accrediting ambassadors to the Community, and new missions or replacements for the ambassadors already in Brussels arrived often. One of the minor concessions granted the French after the boycott was to allow the Commission's wardrobe to be regulated by the governments of the Six. Striped pants, the Six decided, were out. The affair of the striped pants was a new outcropping of an old complaint of the French that the Community was too presumptuous in its conduct of foreign relations and failed to appreciate that the Community cannot have the same competence in its international dealings as does a national government like France. Ergo, it should not display the symbols of parity.

What, then, is the special character of the Community's business-suit diplomat? The nature of the foreign relations of the Community provides an answer. It has been the laborious job of the European Community to dismantle the massive foreign economic relations of the member countries and reconstruct them as the policy of the Community as a whole. The work being done is often as much that of a scholar as that of a diplomat, because the general revision of relations with a country such as the United States, for instance, takes years of study and discussion as in the Kennedy-Round negotiations to reduce tariffs. Sometimes the Community diplomats represent governments, as in the negotiations regarding British membership, and sometimes they represent the Commission, as in the Kennedy-Round negotiations; and the choice depends on what article of the Treaty applies and on how much responsibility the Council will allow the Commission in a given case. To foreign nations the representatives always speak for the Community, however.

Although the foreign policy problems of the Community are no more complex than its internal problems, they are more diffuse. Like the foreign relations of most nations, they lack focus and consist of a group of separate reactions to problems not of the Community's making. Moreover, unlike the pattern of politics that operates within the framework of the Rome Treaty, the foreign politics of the Community can be subject to radical changes overnight. It is possible that the Soviet Union may someday give up its present policy of nonrecognition of the Community, for example, which would immediately revolutionize relations with that government. Knowledge of the Community's present foreign relations is not an entirely perishable commodity, however, because it illuminates the situations facing the Community that circumscribe its alternatives for future action. For instance, there are characteristics of Euro-American economic relations that will endure regardless of the outcome of the Kennedy Round.

Reduced to simplest terms, the foreign policy of the Common Market is (1) to maintain or increase the integrity of the Community and especially to integrate its foreign economic relations, (2) to expand its membership, (3) to gain international recognition and acceptance, and (4) to maintain the special international relationships that have resulted from Europe's traditional preeminence in world trade and from Europe's colonial past. These four objectives are inescapably contradictory, however; and so any policy of the Community that is operationally important has to be some kind of blend of these interests. The goal of integrity conflicts with the other goals of the Community's foreign policy, for instance. On almost all fronts the Community is being pressed to yield on some point of integrity and to extend internal privileges, such as free trading privileges, to outsiders. So many privileges have been distributed to outsiders that it is difficult to define precisely where the Community ends. There is no clear answer to a question like: "Is the group of associated African nations part of the European Community?"

West

The most heated and fateful debate yet to arise in the Community over contradictory policies—in this case a contradiction between integrity and expansion—was the debate over the application of the United Kingdom for membership. Although only six nations were sufficiently interested in the Community to become its original members, other countries of Western Europe were interested in trade liberalization and economic cooperation and were very near to joining. The Scandinavian nations, for instance, had been discussing an economic union ever since the end of the Second World War. The United Kingdom attempted to be included in the free trade arrangements of the Common Market, but this bid was rejected because it would have gained Britain the benefits of the Common Market without her submitting to Community regulations on the internal conduct of her economy.

The immediate alternative for Britain was to form a trading group of its own so as to partially compensate itself for anticipated losses in trade with the Common Market. The ready partners for Britain were those nations of Europe whose trade was already strongly oriented to her, i.e., Portugal, the Scandinavian countries, and the neutral countries of Austria and Switzerland. The British-oriented European Free-Trade Association (EFTA), formed among these seven, was little more than a free-trading partnership and was not intended to be the foundation of a full-blown economic union. Hopes for the new free-trade association were soon dashed when it turned out that its trade with the Common Market was growing faster than trade within the association itself. Adding injury upon injury, the prosperity of the Common Market made it an economic magnet, attracting international capital and talent to the detriment of EFTA industrial expansion.

By 1961, the Macmillan government in Britain had made the fearful choice to apply for admission to the European Community, and some of Britain's EFTA partners applied with her. Negotiations for membership between the Common Market and these lesser neighbors were initiated by formal exchanges of notes, but they were set aside pending conclusion of the negotiations with Britain, the assumption being that whatever fundamental agreement was worked out with Britain would be used as a model for the others. Britain was the strongest bargainer of the group and could demand terms from which all the EFTA applicants could benefit.

At first it appeared as if nothing could stand in the way of British membership in the Common Market, and optimism gripped the participants in the forthcoming negotiations. Lord Edward Heath, the chief British envoy in the negotiations, traveled to Paris to secure the approval of the De Gaulle government for the move and delivered there an eloquent statement of British readiness to merge its destiny with the continent. The whole world looked on in amazement as there seemed to be forming in Europe a new political entity more populous than the United States and, in some ways, more productive. The Six wanted to have EFTA countries join them because they wanted the Community ultimately to unify Europe and not divide it in two.

It was anticipated that fitting Britain into the Common Market would be exceedingly complex, and so facilities for the negotiations were engaged for a two-year period. The negotiations did not last their full term because they were broken off in January, 1963, by the French government, for reasons explained to the world by President de Gaulle in a televised press conference. He said that the British were not ready for the Common Market, referring to them as "Anglo-Saxons" in such a way as to imply an ethnic relationship between Great Britain and the United States that separated it from the continent. The rupture of the negotiations had causes quite extraneous to the negotiations themselves, which were at the brink of success. Simultaneously with the Brussels talks the French government had asked to share British nuclear technology as a gesture in the spirit of community.[1] But the British had to refuse because

[1] Nora Beloff, *The General Says No.* Baltimore, Md.: Penguin Books, 1963, p. 151.

of the treaty restrictions on the technology that had originally been provided by the United States. Concurrently the United States announced its decision to discontinue development of the Skybolt missile, a weapon Great Britain planned to rely upon as her bid to remain an effective member of the nuclear club. Without the Skybolt missile, the British had no effective means of delivering nuclear weapons to a target. President Kennedy met with Prime Minister Macmillan in the Caribbean to agree on an alternative, and there he offered to substitute Polaris missiles for the Skybolt. Later a similar offer was made to the French government, but President de Gaulle rejected it out of hand. To De Gaulle the whole nuclear-weapons affair demonstrated British dependence on America, a dependence that was misplaced, because the United States could not be relied upon to come to the aid of Europe in the case of Soviet attack.

At the time of the rupture several issues still plagued the negotiators in Brussels. One had to do with the methods being devised for harmonizing agricultural policy. On the continent farming was subsidized by fixing high food prices, whereas in England prices were kept low and farmers received direct monetary subsidies. Farmers and consumers alike in Britain feared the consequences of the harmonization. There was no disagreement over the necessity of such a harmonization, but there was strong controversy as to the timing and method of it. There was also the much more difficult problem posed by the British Commonwealth of Nations. Britain could not cut herself free from the special Commonwealth trade pacts because of the bonds of race, nationality, and history that had tied the group together for centuries; but, on the other hand, the Commonwealth could not be admitted to the Common Market without making of it a kind of United Nations for Afro-Asia and Canada. After the suspension of the British negotiations, the EFTA trading partners of Britain withdrew their own bids for membership, feeling that they could not join the market without Britain.

On other fronts the membership question was not all gloomy. In 1961 Greece had become an associate member of the Community under an agreement that would lead to full membership status when her economy attained a high enough level of development; and a similar status was achieved for Turkey in 1964. Spain continued to be tantalized by the prospect of sharing in the riches promoted by the Common Market and applied for association in 1962. But it was politically impossible for a dictatorship to get into the Community. Membership required unanimous approval by the Council of Ministers, a provision expressly included in the Rome Treaty at Dutch insistence to keep dictators out. The Dutch might get support against Spanish admission but would not need it. They can veto. Democratic forces in Spain were stirred up to the point of strikes and demonstrations against the Franco government, in part because Franco disqualified them for membership. In 1966 some minor liberalization of the Spanish regime, including a plan for one–party elections and tacit acceptance of a limited right to strike, coincided with renewed negotiations for association, but to no avail.

It was only a matter of time before the forces for a wider community began to seep around the barricade against Britain and EFTA. First EFTA weakened. There was much grumbling among the members of EFTA that their free-trade area had reached its maximum utility and that further economic advance depended on joining the Common Market.[2] In 1964, the newly elected Labour government in Britain gave its partners in EFTA an unusual present at Christmas time by imposing a fifteen per cent surcharge on all imports into Britain regardless of their origin, trading partner or not. Although favorable economic conditions continued to boost EFTA trade, the British betrayal of EFTA confidence brought criticism upon her from all around her circle.

EFTA members leaned heavily toward joining the Common Market. Although they had unresolved doubts about their ability to switch blocs unless Britain did, Denmark and Ireland held back like coiled springs ready to join the Community the instant Britain's membership seemed assured. Even under the shadow of Soviet–guaranteed neutrality, Austria applied for association with the Community, with which it had the vast majority of its trade. But the President of the Supreme Soviet visited Austria to denounce the step and thus destroy the value of approaching the Common Market on tiptoes. But did the unlikelihood of Soviet armed intervention

[2] Cf. such articles as "Dangers in Europe's Economic Division," *EFTA Reporter*, No. 113, Feb. 8, 1965, p. 1; and "Adverse Effects of Split in Europe," *EFTA Reporter*, No. 122, June 28, 1965, p. 1.

clear the way for application for full membership and the rejection of the Soviet interpretation of neutrality?

Next, the ability of France to prevent British membership in the Common Market was tainted by her overstepping on other issues. When the Common Market was created, the principal initiative had been that of France, who offered European peace, cooperative development, and political unity as the inducements to the other five nations that joined her. Germany and the Benelux nations, however, had to sacrifice their traditional low-tariff policy and some of their anticipated trade with Britain and Scandinavia in order to gain the advantages offered by high-tariff France. Unity with France under De Gaulle was already beginning to appear dubious when in 1965 the Gaullist government affronted its Community partners by boycotting the institutions, like the Soviet Union and South Africa in the United Nations. The Gaullist government considered that the other five had not been cooperating sufficiently with French interests and that they could be forced into line by a spanking. Instead of growing meek, the other five became furious, and the possibility of Britain's joining the five became a theme in speeches on both sides of the Channel. Britain had not joined the original Community because of her long-standing fear of association with the continent. Now, with Britain seriously interested in association with the continent, a switch of the five from France to Britain could possibly entail more gain than loss. The specter of dissolution of the Common Market and its replacement with a new institution including Britain was sufficiently clear to French industrialists that they began criticizing the Gaullist posture. They had invested fortunes in adapting to a giant common market, fortunes they stood to lose if they were forced to market their goods within their own country alone.

When France decided to end the boycott in January, 1966, it was she rather than the others that had to backtrack. The experience did not by itself pave the way for British membership, but it made it possible for any future negotiations on the subject to raise the question, "France or Britain?" The argument that British policy was *too independent* could be applied against British entry into the Common Market only so long as French policy was not equally independent.

The value of widening the circle of Common Market members to embrace all Europe is more easily assumed than defined. *Size* and *unity* are two outstanding values of the new Community, but the two tend to be mutually exclusive where matters of new membership are concerned. To become bigger, the Common Market faces the necessity of sacrificing certain integrating powers and policies in order to suit the national interests of candidate members. And, inversely, as the Common Market becomes more tightly unified, the chances that any outside government would make the adjustments necessary to join it become narrower. In theory, moreover, there was nothing to prevent the Community of Six from rejecting all bids for admission and pursuing integration among themselves and their Greek and Turkish associates alone.

South

Although the Common Market was careful with its dollars, it was spendthrift with its cents. While holding back on new European memberships, the Community quickly extended limited privileges to numerous countries outside Europe. A childhood marriage between the Community and the Afro-Asian world was arranged by the Rome Treaty, under which overseas territories of the Six were "associated" with the Common Market.[3] But with each passing year it became more difficult to predict how the association would turn out, because the attitudes of the parties changed often. At first, the link was merely a logical consequence of the formation of the Common Market. France could not enter a common trading system with the Six without bringing her trading relations with her overseas empire into the bargain. The question of overseas territories was the key and final controversy of the Rome Treaty negotiations, and the result was, in effect, a concession to France.[4] All Six agreed to extend tariff preferences to one another's empires and to contribute handsomely to the development of the colonies through a European Development Fund created for the purpose.

[3] Communauté économique européenne, *Traité instituant la Communauté économique européenne et documents annexes*. Bruxelles, 1957, Arts. 131-136.

[4] Robert Lemaignen, *L'Europe au Berceau*. Paris: Plom, 1964, p. 20.

Thus, with respect to trade and aid, the Belgian, Dutch, French, and Italian empires became the mutual empire of the Community. Then the picture changed.

In 1960, the French, Belgian, and Italian governments gave political independence to the great majority of their African dependencies, and liberty for the rest followed soon afterward. The original terms of association still had until 1963 to run, which left a providential three years to debate the future relationship between Africa and the Community. The three years were just barely enough, because African and European statecraft were in such a state of flux during the early sixties that new commitments of any sort were stalled. At the time of independence a political chain reaction took place. The newly independent nations wanted to assert their autonomy; and, in the wake of a strenuous effort of the Soviet Union and later Red China to establish aid and trade relations with Africa, several African countries tried to keep in the good graces of *both* sides in the Cold War. The reaction in Europe was an immediate campaign of self-ingratiation with Africa. The Community offered to put up $800 million worth of aid.

The subsequent reaction from Africa was somewhat negative. Pan-Africanism, with a strong autarchic streak, was taking hold in capitals across the dark continent. It showed itself first as loose regional unions of African nations, some of which were put aside in 1963, when the continentwide Organization of African Unity was formed. This new organization was to embrace all African nations —new and old, rich and poor, black and white, Christian and Moslem—and its formation was the theoretical and emotional zenith of the Pan-African movement. To Pan-African leaders like former Prime Minister Nkrumah of Ghana, African interests were jeopardized by any hold-over from the old imperial ties with Europe; and the tie with the Common Market was neocolonialism of the worst type. Although the African associates of the Common Market were less fearful than Nkrumah, the road to Addis Ababa, where the Organization of African Unity was formed in May, 1963, afforded little room for the protagonists of the Common Market.

Addis Ababa was a turning point in Pan-Africanism, and the road away was much wider and much smoother. African regionalism became respectable again, and negotiations for a new treaty of association between the Common Market and its French-speaking African partners came to fruition. With the courtship of the African leaders still in full stride, the envoys of the Six traveled to Yaoundé, Cameroon, to sign the new pact in July, 1963. But there was still another political hurdle. Although the association agreement was of some value to all of the Six, it was primarily of value to the French who were thus able to shift to the other five governments some of the burden of development aid and trade preferences for its former African empire.[5] The new convention was included, therefore, among a variety of Common Market measures slowed up by the five in vain as a means of pressing France to drop its opposition to British membership. This slow-up in ratification delayed operation of the convention until July, 1964.

The association established by the treaty of Yaoundé bore marks of permanence. Policy supervision was to be vested in a Council of Association consisting of representatives of all nations concerned, in both Europe and Africa, and the members of the Executive Commission of the Common Market. The program of the association was to be administered by an Association Committee, consisting of a minister from each of the Euro-African associates, which could take formal action by a voting system under which the groups of associates on each side of the Mediterranean had one vote each to cast. No action could be taken, in other words, without the concurrence of both blocs although there might be dissent within one or the other of the blocs. Parliamentary debate of issues of the association was to take place in an annual Parliamentary Conference made up of the members of the European Parliament and representatives of the associated African parliaments. Disagreements over interpretation of the association agreement were to be referred to a special Court of Arbitration whose five members were to be nominated in part by the European associates and in part by the African. The Council held its first annual meeting in Brussels in July, 1964, and set up the Court of Arbitration and Association Committee, dele-

[5] France contributed about one-third of the development fund beginning in 1964 and in 1966 was winning a half of the construction and equipment contracts from the associates.

gating some of its powers to the latter so as to improve the day-by-day oversight of the convention by that committee. The Parliamentary Conference held its first annual meeting in December, 1964, in the Senegalese National Assembly chamber. This array of institutions would have been more impressive had it not been for the fact that many of these same African countries had seen two previous associations with France outfitted with elaborate institutions only to be quickly abandoned, the French Union and the French Community.

Far from being neocolonial in spirit, the convention was a syllabus of benefits for the African partners. Certain tropical products were to be admitted duty free to the European group immediately, and the rest of the African exports were to be brought inside the Common Market's tariff wall by stages. Where African nations needed tariff revenue or needed to protect an infant industry, they did not have to offer tariff reductions reciprocally. The Africans agreed with the Six on the right of establishing businesses in one another's countries, but here too they were allowed to ban European enterprise in order to protect home industry. Finally, the most obvious and immediate benefit was the promise of $800 million of development aid (mostly grants) over a five-year period. After the convention was signed, moreover, the Common Market Council of Ministers agreed to extend to African peanuts the same subsidy that France had previously been paying the producers of that commodity.

The convention favored eighteen former European colonies out of a continent with twice that many countries. Circumstances delayed friction over this favoritism because, although there were African states that competed with the associated nations in sales of cocoa and coffee, the market for those commodities was so good that it absorbed all production. No one was hurt. Banana production in British Cameroon was threatened by unfavorable competition from associated countries, but, when by plebecite the country chose to amalgamate with the former French Cameroon, it came within the preference group. It was clear, however, that in the long run the preferences would damage the trade of the unassociated African nations, particularly Nigeria, and so Nigeria led off a long list of unassociated nations suing for a more equitable relationship with the Common Market. Only the die-hard anti-neocolonial leaders of Ghana and Guinea fought the trend, and their number was reduced by the overthrow of Nkrumah in 1966.

The problem of association with the rest of Africa did not pose so much an *economic* problem for Europe as a *political* one. Europe's African trade was small in proportion to its over-all trade, but the Community wanted friends in Africa. The trouble was that, if the Common Market were to institutionalize relationships with an ever-widening circle of African states, either it would have to drain those relationships of special economic significance or it would have to sacrifice some of its own autonomy and integrity as a self-possessed customs union. How could the Common Market associate with the entire number of its overseas trading partners? The Common Market had to expect to grapple with the problem for years.

Association with the former British colony of Nigeria was concluded in 1966, and other African nations waited in the wings to see what terms Africa's most populous nation could obtain. The association laid down in the Nigerian agreement dealt with trade preferences only, and those were limited. There were no promises of aid from the European Development Fund, and the institutional link was to be a special Council of Association. This association at arm's length seemed to suit the other potential African associates too. The existing African associates, however, were not quite so pleased, although they accepted the agreement.

Asian and Latin American bids for relations were considered suitable for trade agreements only, entailing no organic association. The exclusion was still an arbitrary one, however, and competition in coffee and bananas between the African associates of the Common Market and countries of the Western Hemisphere was likely to breed complaints of injustice in due time. The issue of banana competition broke open at the May, 1966, meeting of the associates in Tananarive, where a Rome Treaty protocol giving Germany a tariff-free quota of bananas was decried by the associates because it was enabling Germany to import Central American bananas as she always had. They felt *they* ought to have the German market. Would the role of Europe in the underdeveloped world ever be a clear one?

Atlantic

There was no tradition of structured trading relations with the United States, but the creation of the Common Market, especially when British membership was in prospect, presented a new situation that called forth proposals for a partnership in trade between Europe and America. The aggregate of foreign trade of the Common Market members was so vast that trading practices adopted jointly by Europe and America would dominate the whole pattern of world trade and could become a tool for world tariff reform. When President Kennedy proposed a partnership, he was not planning new institutions of association between the partners. The two would not be organically tied like business partners; they would merely keep in step, like dancing partners. The world institution for trade cooperation, the General Agreement on Tariffs and Trade (GATT), would provide a framework for extending to its world members any tariff liberalization achieved between the giants.

Since Europe was the best customer of the United States, the formation of the Common Market area was viewed with grave concern by American producers, who feared that European nations would supply ever more of their own needs and reduce their purchases from America. The United States had been actively promoting European integration since the end of the Second World War and was not going to attack the idea of a European customs union per se, but, on the other hand, the United States was not going to stand for unreasonable losses of trade because of the customs union. For its part, the Common Market was concerned about the rapid expansion of American enterprise in Europe and fearful lest American initiative for freer trade should lessen the value of the customs union.[6] The European balance of trade with the United States was unfavorable, moreover, and becoming more unfavorable all the time. If Europe were to move too close to the tremendous industrial and financial power of the United States, it might be taken over economically, like Canada, but much was to be gained on all sides

[6] Allan W. Johnstone in his prize-winning *United States Direct Investment in France*. Cambridge, Mass.: The M.I.T. Press, 1965, finds the fears understandable but groundless.

from a judicious, reciprocal lowering of trade barriers. Moreover, the United States, which had most to gain from tariff reductions, was the guarantor of European military security and Europe's friend in time of need in the past. The American proposal had to be given a sympathetic hearing.

In an effort to simplify the negotiations, the Kennedy administration proposed American legislation that would enable the State Departments to negotiate changes in tariffs by broad categories, as the Common Market wished to do. The Kennedy trade act of 1962 authorized the reduction of American tariffs up to fifty per cent and in certain cases the elimination of tariffs. Small tariffs under five per cent could be eliminated as could tariffs on any article of trade that was eighty per cent accounted for by the two trading giants. This latter authority was left in abeyance by the failure of Britain to gain membership in the Common Market, because without British production, the eighty per cent mark could not be reached for any significant number of commodities. In preliminary talks the Common Market had agreed to the objective of fifty per cent cuts across the board; and, allowing for exceptions, economists predicted an actual achievement of twenty-five per cent.[7]

As the Kennedy-Round negotiations approached during 1963, the spirit of euphoria about Atlantic unity and partnership generated by President Kennedy all evaporated. Anti-American feeling was being nursed in France by the Gaullist regime. The United States had failed to consult Gaullist governments on issues spanning a quarter century, from the Second World War to the Cuban missile quarantine. Rapid Americanization of traditional French social patterns revered by the Gaullists was under way, and American direct investment in France was alarming them. The French politicians who were ready to cry "enough!" to America were being applauded at home. De Gaulle was said to regard the Kennedy Round as an American attempt at economic take-over.[8]

In 1964 the "chicken war" broke out. The erection of a common tariff wall against American frozen chickens helped establish a frozen chicken industry in Europe that supplanted American sales

[7] Stanley D. Metzger, *Trade Agreements and the Kennedy-Round*. Fairfax, Va.: Coiner Publications, 1964, p. 101.

[8] Beloff, *op. cit.*, p. 38.

overnight. From the American standpoint, a tariff so discriminating against American exporters should not have been imposed arbitrarily, and, if it were maintained, the United States had the right to retaliate. From the European point of view, the United States had the right to retaliate, that was one of the anticipated prices of the Common Market, but the Americans could not retaliate for the *whole value* of the lost chicken sales. In Europe frozen chickens was an infant industry, but it would have displaced many American sales eventually even in the absence of any tariff change. Moreover, European imports of feed grain from the United States were being increased to feed Europe's chickens. Could the United States be so fussy about the form in which it shipped its protein to Europe?

Only a tiny fraction of American trade was involved in the issue. But the eyes of the world were upon it because it illustrated how conflicts over the evolution of the Common Market were going to be handled. The Common Market retained its chicken wall, and the United States raised the tariff on goods originating from the Common Market countries concerned in proportion to the amount of chicken sales lost in each. A GATT committee arbitrated the amount of retaliation. Both sides were pinching pennies.

Lost markets for industrial goods had caused foreign complaints from the very start of the Common Market. In 1959, in order to compensate injured parties, the Common Market renegotiated tariff concessions its members had made to outside parties previously. And when a subsequent reduction was made in the Community's internal tariff, that same reduction was offered unilaterally to the world. Later, in 1962, an agreement was made to reduce the target tariff of the Community to twenty per cent below the arithmetical average of community tariffs in exchange for comparable concessions by the Community's trading partners. The Community was thus making an effort to avoid the pitfalls of autarchy and to compensate its trading partners for their newly lost markets.

But these concessions affected industrial markets only, and, as the Community's agricultural policy began to take shape, it brought back the complaints of injustice in even more virulent form. The new Community regulations required all food from unassociated nations to compete with European food at a disadvantage; and so, presumably, some further compensation for ruined markets was in order. But, to the chagrin of the Americans, the Common Market, fresh from the heat of the chicken war, took the offensive in the Kennedy Round. It complained that the United States was afforded unjustified protection by certain high tariffs and insisted upon a formula that would reduce exceptionally high tariffs more than low tariffs. Thus, according to a European proposal, if there were a target tariff of ten per cent, a high tariff of thirty per cent would be reduced by fifty per cent of the difference from the target (i.e., down to twenty per cent), while existing tariffs of ten per cent or lower would not be lowered at all. As for tariffs on food, the Common Market proposed to bring the whole trading world into a new regime by which farm production and prices, including those in Europe, could be protected.

The Kennedy Round seemed doomed from the start. The Americans could not see any provocation for the Common Market's demands. The over-all tariff schedule of the United States was not higher than the European. It was lower if one considered the volume of European goods that entered the United States under one of its numerous low tariffs. As for the high tariffs, the Americans had thought themselves generous in proposing to cut these drastically. Fifty per cent made a bigger dent in a high tariff than a low tariff. Certainly there was going to be a greater impact on American buyers of, say, German sail boats if they could enter the United States market at prices fifteen per cent lower than before any Kennedy-Round tariff cuts, while American rugs enter the Common Market at only a faintly lower price. There was an inevitable amount of guesswork in the opinions of economists on both sides of the Atlantic, however, when it came to estimating how many sales were being stopped by given tariffs, there having never been a tariff-free period for comparison.

There were political overtones in the approach taken by the Common Market. From the standpoint of some Europeans, if the Americans wanted a partnership, it had to be a general partnership and not merely a trading partnership. Why not promote along with the economic partnership a political partnership in the management of Western defense and the control of nuclear weapons? But the Kennedy Round was not an adequate framework to discuss such sweeping issues, and perhaps for that reason they thought an agreement might be postponed until satisfaction on the other counts was achieved in NATO talks or elsewhere.

The European negotiators complained about American nontariff obstacles to trade that differed from standards laid down in the GATT agreements. They did not like certain tariffs being determined on the basis of the American selling price of articles similar to those imported, rather than on the actual price of the imports, for instance. Another complaint was against the so called "buy-American" legislation, which dated from the 1930's and which had been magnified in significance more recently by huge governmental outlays for foreign military operations. The purchase of supplies for United States forces abroad and soldiers' spending on leave abroad had become potential threats to the American balance of payments, making it particularly hard in the Kennedy Round for the United States to loosen up its buy-American restrictions on government procurement. The Europeans cited the fact that they buy from America nearly twice as much as they sell to it as an argument justifying concessions from America. But the great disparity in Atlantic trade was made possible by the vast infusion of dollars into Europe through American investments and military operations there, dollars that found their way back to the United States in payment for rapidly increasing European purchases.

The balance of payments had been unfavorable for the United States despite its huge favorable trade balance. If Atlantic trade were to be *in balance,* compensating measures would have to be taken to prevent the cost of American forces in Europe from draining out America's gold stocks. Failing such measures, however, from the point of view of an American Congressman, any American tariff or investment advantages over Europe constituted a form of indirect taxation to help support the NATO force in lieu of unattainable appropriations from other NATO countries.

The key problem of the Kennedy Round was agricultural tariffs. The Common Market proposed that world commodity agreements be negotiated for grain and a few other key commodities that would freeze all national agricultural support measures at their existing levels and establish world prices for the commodities concerned. The United States was willing to accept the principle of world commodity agreements but differed radically from the Common Market on prices. From the point of view of the United States, too high a grain price in Europe would destroy a large part of the traditional market for American food there, while protecting uneconomic farming in Europe. The Americans argued for the entry of their cheaper food into Europe on the ground that the whole world profited from specialization in production. If the United States was better fitted because of its huge land area to produce certain crops cheaply, then protectionism should not be allowed to interfere. From the Common Market's point of view, to let the United States through the food tariff wall could upset the agricultural objectives of the Community. The Community had counted on free trade in food internally to promote modernization, specialization, self-sufficiency, and economies of size. Much of European agriculture had yet to be modernized and, if promoted properly, could possibly be as efficient as American farming. European food trade was therefore insulated from the outside world by means of trade restrictions insuring that foreign prices would be kept slightly above Common Market prices. In some commodities European demand outstripped European supply, and there was a market for foreign food. But the European produce always had priority in the market place. American sales fell off, such as the sales in flour, which disappeared except for some small sales to the Netherlands. But did not Europe have a right to fulfill its agricultural potentialities, even though history had blessed American farming with modernization first?

With no successes registered in the Kennedy Round between 1962 and 1966, the factors appeared to blur into hopeless deadlock. Extraordinary patience was being shown, but something had to happen eventually. The mere creation of the Common Market was viewed by third parties as discrimination, and hopefully that was going to be remedied by reforms adopted in the Kennedy Round and *not* remedied by tariff retaliation. In a tariff war all sides would suffer. The Common Market could thus maintain its integrity, but at a price, because European wealth was based so much on trade. Therefore, trading partners such as the United States might have to be given easier access to the European market, but how easy? The Americans were willing to absorb certain trade losses in order to promote European unity, but how much loss could

they consent to? Add to these questions the numerous considerations raised by other GATT member nations in the negotiations
and one saw the elements of some of the most complicated diplomacy of our time, perhaps too complicated to have any hope of
success.

The De Gaulle boycott in 1965 interrupted the Kennedy Round,
because the Common Market could not meet to decide on its positions. With several of their nine lives used up, the negotiations
resumed again after the settlement of the Common Market's agricultural policy in July, 1966. But by then the time was at hand
when Congress would have to renew the five-year negotiating authority it had enacted in 1962. Since the Common Market had
made so little headway during the five years, American negotiators
were undecided as to whether they should even request a renewal.

East

The Common Market was not the only grouping of nations wor-
ried about safeguarding its integrity. The satellite relationship of
Eastern European countries with the Soviet Union began to thaw
during the Khrushchev era and allow an increase in trade with
Western Europe. The concurrent emergence of the Common Market multiplied the threat to Communist bloc solidarity and produced in the Soviet Union an acute though innocuous hostility that
promised to postpone regular relations between the Soviet and
Western trading blocs indefinitely.

The Soviets were being pinched from three directions. First, the
Soviet government was habitually sensitive to progress toward Western European integration since each such success tended to tip the
balance in East-West competition in favor of the West. Second, the
Soviet Union stood to lose effectiveness in its use of foreign trade
for international political purposes. The Soviets could induce individual countries to accept low-priced subsidized Soviet oil, for example, and thus upset the pattern of Western oil trade; but the
Common Market was slated to take over the commercial policy
for all member countries in time and could be strong enough to
control Soviet dumping. Finally, the Common Market was becom-

ing increasingly seductive to nations of the Red bloc, because it was being credited with the burgeoning prosperity of Western Europe in the sixties. The increased trade across the Iron Curtain threatened in the long run to create some dependence by the Eastern European countries on Western markets and to lead to some degree of reorientation away from Moscow.

The first inclination of the Russians was to deny the legal existence of the Common Market and to insist that all tariff reductions among the Six should be extended to the Soviet Union in accordance with the most-favored-nation principle. Why should Germany have any better tariff rates from France than the Soviet Union? The Soviets were able to prop up their bilateral trading with Western Europe by signing new trade agreements, but that prop threatened to disappear when the Common Market took over trade-agreement writing as provided under the Rome Treaty.

Nonrecognition of the Common Market gave the Soviets a little grist for their propaganda effort among nations of the Southern Hemisphere that thought the Common Market worked against them. But the Russians may have anticipated having to reconcile themselves to the Common Market sooner or later, and it was hinted during 1962 that it might be sooner. At that time Premier Khrushchev made a vague statement about the "possibility of economic collaboration . . . not only between individual states . . . but also between their economic associations." [9] In an oblique way, this statement seemed not only to recognize the existence of the Common Market but also to point out some future value in organized relations between it and Comecon, the East European economic association. Soon again Soviet statements referring to the Common Market resumed their invective. But behind their condemnation of the Common Market the Soviet authorities engaged in the kind of byplay with the Community that hinted at possible future collaboration. In 1962 during Franco-Russian negotiations for a new trade agreement, Russian demands for the same tariff concessions France was giving to her Common Market partners caused a rupture of the talks. The next year the Soviet government addressed letters to each of the members of the Common Market

[9] Published in *Problems of Peace and Socialism*. Prague, September, 1962.

asking for most-favored-nation treatment, only to be told by all in identical language that Soviet authorities would have to address their entreaty to the Commission in Brussels, because individual Common Market members no longer set their own external tariffs. The Soviet government did not take this advice, but in 1964 Soviet officials began looking Brussels over and quietly investigating the mechanical problems involved in establishing an embassy to the European Community.[10] That same year the Council of Ministers addressed a note to the Soviet government expressing its willingness to grant tariff concessions sought by the Soviets if that government would enter into negotiations with the Executive Commission, but the Soviets did not answer.

Whether any of these gestures would have useful consequences remained an unanswerable question that hinged on several issues extraneous to the European Community, such as the Chinese charges against Soviet "capitalism," the ideological implications of the anti-Khrushchev coup in Russia, and Soviet assessments as to whether sunshine or chilling winds were best able to remove the cloak of solidarity from the West. The Soviet government wanted to accelerate economic growth by purchasing large quantities of technical equipment in Western Europe, but it needed the foreign exchange it could get from the sale of its products in the West. And to have increased sales of Russian caviar, for example, would have required tariff concessions that only the Common Market could give. Whether this factor counted for much was open to doubt, because the Soviets could buy with gold from their huge stocks. And in the past that government had been willing to lose money in order to dump items like low-price oil across high tariff walls in Europe for political purposes.

The Common Market had more to gain than the Soviets in the establishment of relations. The resulting increase in trade would be more benefit to the Europeans who depended on trade than to the Soviets who depended primarily on domestic materials and markets. And, acting together through the Common Market, the Western partners would have been able to counteract some of the politically motivated Soviet trading techniques that had had dis-

[10] *New York Times,* May 6, 1964.

ruptive effects on West European nations. Soviet reconciliation with the Common Market would probably have to have had a political motive, but the Community saw no harm in trying to purchase Soviet goodwill by offering tariff breaks.

If the Common Market were to have broken up, it would *not* have been because of Soviet nonrecognition, and the remoteness of a breakup made the Soviet policy look hopeless. The Soviet Union had only to admit this to itself and accept the generous trade offer made by the Community. But the Russians were so sensitive about the possibility of the thaw causing Soviet bloc nations to lean toward the West that it began a vigorous revival of the long dormant Comecon organization that worked to tie the Eastern European economies to one another by common planning, common transportation and power networks, and mutual financing of development. Possibly the Soviets reasoned that they should prepare to come to terms with the Common Market by integrating the Eastern European economies so tightly that they could not help but function as a unit indefinitely. But they were due to be disappointed, because the idea of a tighter Comecon based on specialization of industry was distasteful to Roumania, for instance, who saw herself being made the bread basket for industrialized Czechoslovakia and denounced the principle of leadership from Moscow.[11] Economic nationalism outshone Comecon in Eastern Europe.

There was no immediate possibility that the Eastern European countries would switch blocs, because, aside from the immense political power wielded by the Soviet Union in each of those countries, the Common Market could not make ties with them for the duration of the Hallstein doctrine. While heading the German foreign office, the same Walter Hallstein that came to be Common Market Commission president enunciated the policy that the Federal Republic would not have diplomatic relations with any country that recognized Communist East Germany, as the whole Communist world did. Since Germany was a member of the Common Market and could veto any form of association with Eastern

[11] Zbigniew K. Brzezinski, The Soviet Bloc, the Common Market, and France, in *France and the European Community*, Sydney N. Fisher, ed. Columbus, O.: Ohio State University Press, 1964, p. 154.

European countries, there was no association feasible, even with such an independent Communist country as Yugoslavia. Moreover, the new leaders of the Soviet Union that succeeded Khrushchev in October of 1964 gave no indication that they would change the policy of their government toward the Common Market.

The Misfit

It is hard to overstate the importance the Common Market ascribes to its foreign trade relations. And the great care being shown in the revamping of Europe's foreign economic relations results, generally, in delay. Hence, by the end of nine years the Community had made trade agreements with specific nations and associations with Greece and Turkey and one group of African states, but it had yet to work out all the most critical areas of its foreign relations. No new members had joined, many questions regarding Europe's economic relations with underdeveloped countries remained unanswered, the Kennedy Round had borne no fruit, and there were no relations with the Soviet bloc.

The Europhiles that emphasize the internal European bonds that favor federation are apt to ignore the fact that regional integration automatically severs external bonds, which have to be retied to the regional entity in a new way. The Common Market has fitted into international relations especially slowly for two reasons. Everything about the foreign relations of a regional union is strange and new and is being worked out by the Community for the first time in modern history. Other regional unions, if such do come in other parts of the world, may benefit from the example. But more important, Europe is no ordinary trading bloc. It makes a difference whether the Community has Britain as a member or not, but, speaking generally, the European Community is very nearly the center of the entire trading world. To revamp and integrate the foreign economic relations of the Six is, in effect, to revamp the economic relations of most of the world. It remains to be seen whether it will be possible for the Common Market to settle its foreign policy as if it were just another new nation. It may falter, and the foreign economic policy of the Six may remain divided and in national hands. Or it may find increasing need to settle economic questions it has raised, by means of worldwide agreements like some it has already suggested in the Kennedy Round. What started out to be the establishment of integrated economic relations for one region could result instead in a new approach to the international commercial problems of the whole world.

Reverberations

IX

The creation of the Common Market may prove to have been one of the greatest diplomatic accomplishments of the latter half of the twentieth century. Such an accomplishment reverberates throughout the political world, and part of any accurate image of the Common Market includes its image as reflected in its emulators and the shadow it casts over other human enterprises and over its own future.

Europe and the World

The most elegant testimony to the spell of the European Community was the rapidity with which other groups of nations moved to copy the venture. The Central American Common Market, the Latin American Common Market, the West African Common Market, the Arab Common Market, the European Free Trade Association, and Comecon have all copied certain features of the European Community.[1] These other groups view European successes as a promise for their success, and some of them have invoked the charm of the Common Market name to bless their efforts. The European Common Market is basically different from them, how-

[1] Comecon reaction to West European integration dates from the Marshall Plan, but it was dormant until the rise of Khrushchev and of the Common Market.

ever. It was established among nations that were one another's best customers, whereas some of the imitations are among nations with little history of mutual trade. The European countries used existing trade to justify removing tariff barriers and enacting common economic legislation. The imitations intend the reverse, to remove the barriers to trade that did not exist in order to create trade. Whether imitations will work or not does not detract from the fact that the common-market idea has spread throughout the continents, for good or for ill. European ideas in general have been distrusted outside Europe as being neocolonial, but the idea of the European Common Market is an exception.

All of the common markets want to develop to the size at which they can be competitive with the other economic giants of the world, and they desire political unity. Regional political organizations existed before, in the Organization of American States and the Arab League, for example, but the common-market idea appeared to be the first tangible step by which those loosely associated regions could unify further. The new nations have not even waited to see if Europe would succeed before starting their own experiments.

At the same time, antagonism has developed between the Common Market and the United Nations. And, quite apart from the effectiveness and inspiration that have graced the endeavors of the Common Market, it has come to look pernicious in some foreign eyes. The antagonism has three facets, historical, intellectual, and economic, and of the three the economic is the most worrisome. None of the antagonisms have to exist, however. The Common Market and the regionalist projects that have drawn inspiration from it have rekindled an old argument. In the closing months of the Second World War when the postwar world was being planned, the two dominant personalities of that time, Roosevelt and Churchill, advanced contrary plans for peace. Churchill's would have divided the world among regional unions that would be coordinated by a Supreme World Council. And Roosevelt's, weakly echoed from Moscow, envisaged a world organization within which a great-power police force would maintain peace.[2] Roosevelt's plan prevailed, and, at that time, outside of Europe the only new

[2] Both plans are discussed in Ruth B. Russell, *History of the United Nations Charter*. Washington, D.C.: The Brookings Institution, 1958, pp. 96-109.

regionalist stirring was the Arab League. In the years to come the United Nations helped regional systems to succeed. The Middle East was at the point of fratricide on a number of occasions when the United Nations stepped in to restore stability. United Nations action in the Congo was decisive in preventing Africa from dividing into warring camps. And it was the United Nations Economic Commission for Latin America that established the Latin American Common Market.

The more recent emergence of regionalism around the world gives the appearance that it threatens the United Nations as the organizing framework of international relations. Although the contest was a real one historically during the war, there is no conflict in theory between the universalism of the United Nations and the regionalism of the Common Market. Look at the matter in hypothetical terms. If the goal of regional union were achieved throughout the continents, world politics might become vastly simpler, and there might not be enough major communities of nations to fill all fifteen seats of the United Nations Security Council! Whether the coalescence of the members of the United Nations into a few larger entities would lessen in any way the frictions that have existed in that body would be difficult to say. Just as the nation states once unified warring baronies and suppressed internal dissension, new regional unions could overcome *their* internal squabbles; but the main frictions in the United Nations have existed *between* the huge nations like the United States and the Soviet Union, not within them.

No functions of the United Nations need be preempted by regional unions. The United Nations would have no competitor as peace-keeper. It could still be a channel for economic equalization among the regions just as it always has been, because unification alone could not make the Southern regions rich. Thus with its membership smaller and organizational puzzles less complicated, the United Nations might emerge after the successful organization of regional unions as a more efficient and more important organization than before.

Success in the European Community, moreover, gives no guarantee of the success of regional unions in other parts of the world.

If Europe alone were successful in unifying, there might be little impact on international organizations other than to reduce Europe's representation to one delegation in the United Nations, in NATO, and in any other organizations with membership wider than Europe; and Europe might never attain that degree of integration *itself*.

The popular interest excited by the European Community has caused an unfortunate response among some of the Europhile intelligentsia that is productive of a spurious intellectual antagonism between the European Community and the United Nations.[3] The antagonism is based on the dubious assumption that success in a smaller venture is of greater value than a less fruitful struggle in a larger venture. The Europeans have shown originality in their pattern of integration, and their message for international organization will be treated in the section below. But Community officials and European academicians have evidenced blindness to the special circumstances that facilitated European integration. Old, tired, dispirited, doleful, failing—these are the adjectives that color their discussion of the United Nations. Structural differences between the Common Market and the United Nations have been exaggerated so as to place the Common Market in a different and higher class. The deprecation of the United Nations may play a useful psychological role for Europeans, but logically this class-conscious type of antagonism is artificial. How can the Common Market's success in abolishing internal trade barriers be of any help in such problems as mounting a 25,000-man peace force for the vast and delicate Congo mission? Beyond its banking operations the Common Market does not conduct administrative enterprises. Even in the matter of structural advances the Common Market cannot assert superiority, because it retains the principle of unanimous voting in many cases and the United Nations does not. The Common Market showed itself to be weaker than the state of Luxembourg in the controversy over the location of the Community's headquarters, whereas it is unlikely that the United Nations could be deterred by opposition of

[3] A debate among some of the most highly placed exponents of the two sides can be read in Alan Burr Overstreet, "The Nature and Prospects of European Institutions: A Report on the Second Carnegie Endowment Conference on International Organization," *Journal of Common Market Studies*, III, 1965, 124-168.

that nature to one of its decisions. Nor has the United Nations neared perdition because of the intransigence of one of its members.

The economic antagonism between the Common Market and the United Nations is real, and varying degrees of vilification of the Common Market have been expressed in United Nations debates. The complaints originate in the economic exclusiveness the Community has shown toward the underdeveloped countries of the world—exclusiveness as to which ones it will associate with, as to which ones it will aid, and as to the manner in which decisions in this connection are to be taken. In strengthening its economic integrity the Community has strengthened its hand in relation to its Afro-Asian and Latin American trading partners, who have always had weak bargaining positions in the past anyway. The United Nations, on the other hand, provides a policy-making framework in which there is little possibility of exclusivism and where the underdeveloped countries have a voice.

The Common Market has come some distance in trying to relieve its antagonism to the United Nations. First of all it has conducted an information program designed to mellow the issue and reassure the governments that felt injured that an acceptable arrangement would be worked out. Second, it has tried to show in its association agreements with African nations that it does not intend to use its cumulative economic power to impose exploitive terms on weaker nations. As a result, the fears in some areas have abated.[4] On the initiative of underdeveloped nations an attempt has been made to induce the members of the Common Market and other developed nations to solve within the framework of the United Nations the trade problems bearing on economic development. The United Nations Conference on Trade and Development was called into session repeatedly after 1964 for this purpose, but with scant success. The Common Market nations may be justified in their reticence toward the Conference, but one can appreciate why the new nations—so numerous and so poor—may visualize the United Nations as "mine" and the Common Market as "thine."

[4] A case study in this pattern of changing attitudes is found in Rouhollah K. Ramazani, *The Middle East and the Common Market.* Charlottesville, Va.: University Press of Virginia, 1964.

Europe and Parliamentary Diplomacy[5]

The increasing number of nations and the multiplication of international relations has in the present century exceeded the utility of traditional, capital to capital, diplomacy and has called forth the international organization, which is at base a rationalizing framework for conferences or congressional diplomacy. In modern European history, when the rise of liberal democracy made it necessary to relate many voices to the governing process, a rational technique for doing so evolved and crystallized in the institution called the parliament (literally the *consultation*). Now, as international organizations seek to emerge from their primitive infancy, they are testing ways of rationalizing consultations within *their* councils and assemblies. And they have as a yardstick the successes already demonstrated by national parliaments in relating numerous interests to the policy making process, weighting their representation, polishing their procedure, facilitating the resolution of differences, and taking action.

The experience of the European Community has been a creative experience for the whole diplomatic world because of the advances it has registered in organizing or rationalizing decision making. Parliamentary methods have advanced into the procedures of the Community in three outstanding ways, and in these ways the Community is a leader and a model of what is possible for other international organizations.[6] First, the voting formulas of the Council of Ministers have moved far in the direction of majority rule, which is the cornerstone of parliamentary decision making. The Treaty defined certain types of regulations that could be adopted by less than all of the Ministers, even if an opponent represented a major

[5] Viewing the problem of modern diplomacy as a problem in parliamentary forms has been stimulated by such writings as Dean Rusk, Parliamentary Diplomacy—Debate v. Negotiation, *World Affairs Interpreter*, Vol. XXVI, No. 2 (summer, 1955), pp. 121-122; and Philip Jessup, Parliamentary Diplomacy, *Recueil des Cours*, Vol. LXXXIX-I. Leyden: Sythoff, 1956, pp. 185-319.

[6] The term *international organization* is used here to refer in theory to all international institutions from those with the meagerest symbols of integrity to those that are almost, but not quite, federations.

power, and there is as yet no international organization outside the
Community that can adopt compulsory regulations in such a way.[7]

Second, the European Community includes a parliament of the
classic type among its institutions, although it has little more than
an advisory role. And this unit conducts a permanent campaign
to introduce additional parliamentary methods into Community
activity. Other European organizations have parliaments too, or,
like NATO, have debated having one. The United Nations, because of disunity and the numerous dictatorships among its members is far from ready for a parliament. Still, the United Nations
has never been completely free of the spell of parliamentarism.
Even before the European parliaments were created after the Second
World War, governments included members of their parliaments
in their delegations to the United Nations. Also, the veto in the
Security Council relates voting there to population more closely
than did the principle of sovereign equality that governed earlier
voting formulas, and it is in that degree a step in the direction of
parliamentarism. The one-nation-one-vote principle has been called
under question in the United Nations, especially since the emergence of numerous splinter nations from the erstwhile colonial
empires, and that has shown a sensitivity for parliamentary standards of representation. Also, members of the United Nations have
formed caucusing groups that mirror the role of political groups
in parliaments.

Third, the European institutions have *internalized* their procedures. United Nations procedures, by contrast, have remained
largely *externalized*. The essential work of the Council of Ministers,
the Commission, and the European Parliament is prepared methodically *within* their formal framework and does not burst upon the
scene in the form of proposals by national delegations, fought for
behind the scenes in informal groups or through makeshift channels

---

[7] The key word is *regulation*. Other organizations either employ the *convention* as a means of establishing a new regime (and the convention would
bind only its signatories) or adopt a regulation by majority vote with the
proviso that any member can choose to be exempted from it within a time
limit. Mandatory action can be voted by a majority of either the Security Council of the United Nations or the Organ of Consultation of the Rio Pact, but
such acts are specific. They are not new laws in the sense of permanently
prescribed patterns of action.

of communication. The value of formal methods of decision making is their efficiency. But why should one organization succeed in erecting a more inclusive decision-making framework than another? *Size, compulsion,* and *consensus* provided an answer. A policy-making subcommittee of the Common Market needs only six faces at its table to represent all its members. The United Nations, on the other hand, has had to deal with a problem of exclusiveness in most of its committees. The Economic and Social Council is a preparatory organ of the General Assembly, but since only one-quarter of the United Nations members can be members of it at one time, it has been timid and thus lost efficiency. Exclusiveness has caused jealousy in the organization, and the Charter has been amended to increase the Council's size. Lacking exclusive committees that are trusted by the general membership, the United Nations can do little important preparatory work within its formal structure.

The binding character of the Common Market's decisions has been partly responsible for its measured care in decision making. Participation in a series of formal reviews of a proposal is a member's main guarantee that its interests will be respected. On the other hand, since the resolutions of the United Nations General Assembly do not bind any member, the passage of a hastily conceived resolution is not so serious. If by casually putting together the principles that appeal to various voting blocs one can muster enough votes to pass a resolution, why not do it? Such a question could not arise in the Common Market where every decision of the Council compels compliance and must be carefully perfected beforehand.

The members of the Common Market have had differences of opinion, but they have not sought one another's downfall. Their differences are encompassed within a framework of consensus. On the other hand, in organizations stultified by the Cold War, like the United Nations, there can be little fruitful negotiation at lower levels. On points of Cold War differences the positions of governments are hardened, and no amount of preliminary committee work can be of any avail. There is nothing to do but arrange support for a measure in the corridors, submit it to the plenary organ or its main committees—possibly getting some surprise or propaganda value—and square off for the vote. Corridor diplo-

macy is used in the United Nations as an expedient, although there
is nothing inherently desirable in corridor diplomacy. The issue
of closed versus open diplomacy is not posed here because there
is no question of bringing United Nations diplomacy out of the
corridors and into the open. The question is whether it can be
brought into the realm of routine and experience and out of the
realm of intrigue and accident.

Europe and Its Governments

The European Community is having an effect upon European
governments. Although the effect is difficult to define, the study
of European governments, by American scholars at least, is taking
the Community ever more into account.[8] The change being brought
about lies in the absorption of power by the Community, although
the absorption so far has not been great. The member nations
have not needed to modify their constitutional procedures and
institutions, and some may never need to do so other than to
satisfy some local desire. One cannot expect a shortening of the
agendas of the national parliaments because of the European Community; there was no shortening of the agendas of State legislatures
in America when Federal activities in that country were enlarged.
A federal jurisdiction takes on essentially *new* problems peculiar
to its own objectives, leaving the existing legislatures with their
existing problems. There is no essential conflict, and both levels
can spend more money and make more decisions every year. But
the two levels change in relative importance.

The European Community was created where nothing existed
before, and it exists preeminently to do the things the European
nations had never done and could never do on their own. Before
there was a European entity there could be little development of
nuclear energy for peaceful purposes or astronautical development.
Almost every kind of industry was denied its potentialities—processed cheese, kitchen appliances, knitting, residential heating. In-

[8] For example, the Community was treated as one of six key European governments in Clifford A. L. Rich *et al, European Politics and Government.* New
York: Ronald Press, 1962.

ventive or research-oriented industries could hardly exist at all, and there was no poverty program. European institutions have now provided a framework for the retraining and reemployment of displaced workers, whereas national governments had not. And the plans to coordinate the social legislation of the Community members have opened up a new policy area that overlies and does not supplant national policy making. There is a parallel with the United States here in that the American state governments have committed themselves ever more deeply to social welfare, and at the same time the Federal government has enacted a growing social welfare system that overlies the state programs. In due time, too, the European Community might absorb the bureaus and functions of the multitude of specialized European organizations dealing with international problems like the delivery of mail, the detection of fugitives from justice, and the mapping of motor routes. If it would necessitate European institutions to sponsor competitive commercial aircraft and merchant ships and all other things needful and characteristic of a vast new political entity, eventually those institutions could assume such responsibilities too. The Community *could* be Europe's touch with greatness if it were given the chance.

There has had to be some displacing of national jurisdiction by European institutions, notably over tariff and agricultural policy, but those are special cases. The tariffs had to be eliminated along with the other arbitrary barriers between the member nations and a new external tariff erected by the Community, for instance. Europe could not have become a unit otherwise. Coordination of most other subjects of public policy would not necessarily entail such direct uprooting of decision-making authority from the national parliaments.

Europe and Its Future

The future of the European Community is continually under discussion in Europe, and the discussions have touched on all the key ways in which the Community might develop. There is much about the present Community that cannot basically change. Not much can be done to modify the classic design of the Parliament the Community already has, although the powers and political base of the Parliament could be enlarged. And since collegiate executives are habitual in European constitutional practice, no basic change can be expected in the structure of the Commission, although its powers and method of election might change. Also the European Court finds itself in classic form, although still lacking in some jurisdiction and in an appeals mechanism. If there is to be a continued representation of states in the Community, the life of the Council of Ministers might be prolonged, although possibly with different powers and personnel. It becomes difficult to conceive of radically different European institutions without delving into possibilities that would appear farfetched from the European point of view.

Possibly none of the proposals for developing the Community toward federal union will materialize, either because of a general failure of will to integrate or because some other and better plan emerges. But two types of proposals have been set forth persistently. The proposal most widely discussed was the French proposal emanating from a committee set up by the European head of state under the chairmanship of the French delegate Christian Fouchet, a confidant of De Gaulle's. The Fouchet Plan was the basis of discussion of European union because it was the lowest common denominator among the various approaches to the problem. It was the smallest step that the European Community could take toward political unity, and discussion centered on whether or not the proposal was too weak. No one considered it too strong. There was no other practical way of approaching the matter, because the French government under President de Gaulle could be expected to veto any stronger proposal. The French President appeared proud of his having made possible the submission of the Fouchet Plan and cited the Plan as proof of his unflagging devotion to the ideal of European unity.

The Plan was calculated to add new functions to the existing ones of the Community, but it demanded a price for the step. The gains were to be these: There would have been created, under the Fouchet Plan, a new Council within which the heads of governments of the Six would meet at widely spaced intervals to discuss political questions, particularly foreign policy. The European Parliament would have the right to communicate with this new institution (but no power over it), and the new Council would be served by its own secretariat. The Council could make engagements that were binding on all members by unanimous vote. The Six were free already to make such engagements any time they wished, but the Fouchet Plan would have made the contacts more regular. The Plan imposed no specific obligations on the new Council, which left open the possibility that it might not come to agreement on any foreign policy, ever.

The price to be exacted was this: At first the Plan asked to have the new body seated in Paris, which might have tipped the choice of a European capital in favor of Paris. But this point was dropped almost immediately in a revision of the proposal prepared by Fouchet.[9] Paris might eventually become the seat of the Community, but the French would have to bargain more subtlely. Also, the new framework was to be set up separately from the existing institutions. There would be no way that the existing Community could prevent the new Council of heads of government from draining off any issue from their agenda that some head of government regarded as political. In effect, the new Council could practically guarantee that the existing European Community would never have the muscle-building experience of working and fighting over a major issue. The new Council could put the old Council in its place. What the Fouchet Plan was conspicuously avoiding was any attempt to strengthen the existing Community. Conceivably a procedure could be established by which heads of government could sit within the framework of the existing Council of Ministers, whose powers could be broadened, but that was not suggested by the Plan.

The second plan for Europe's future was more of an idea than a blueprint. It envisaged the development of the existing Community into the realm of top-level policy making, including foreign policy making, and the perfection of the European Parliament by establishing direct popular elections and by giving it real powers over the other Community organs. The most assiduous exponent of the creation of a political union out of the existing Community

[9] See the concordance in European Parliament, Political Committee, *Towards Political Union*. Luxembourg, 1964, p. XIV.

was the government of the Netherlands. And the Dutch delegates were the most vitriolic in their denunciation of the French position on political union. There was sympathy for the Dutch position among all members of the Fouchet Committee except Fouchet himself. And President Hallstein liked to point out that the Common Market already *was* a political community, albeit in need of strengthening, and that mischief could be done by creating an artificial dichotomy between economics and politics in two separate communities.

The Belgian foreign minister played the part of mediator between the Dutch and the French. Belgium had staunchly supported steps toward unity but feared that, if political union came too soon, Britain would never join. The Dutch accepted that, but their disagreement over the Fouchet Plan caused a permanent rupture of negotiations in April, 1962. In May of 1962, De Gaulle said at a press conference that the partners could not expect both to have a tighter Community *and* to have Britain join, because of what he considered to be British aversion for supranational institutions. Hence, there was to be a holiday in advances toward a political community. He did not mention at the time, however, that he was also going to block British membership.

De Gaulle's plan for political union took the form, in September, 1962, of a treaty of cooperation with Germany alone. German Chancellor Adenauer had developed an admiration for the German-speaking De Gaulle, and some fruitful forms of cooperation appeared imminent. The substance of the treaty evaporated very quickly, however, when it became plain that by cooperation De Gaulle had meant subservience to French policy. In 1964, Belgian, German, and Italian speeches and draft proposals offering modified and strengthened versions of the Fouchet Plan were circulated among the governments. And on May 9, 1965, the anniversary of the Schuman Plan declaration, German Chancellor Erhard made a new appeal for "the organization of Europe [to] . . . meet the demands of the modern world." "Europe must arrive at a joint policy," he said, "in the fields of economy, research, defense, and foreign policy." But within a few weeks, the French had walked out of the Common Market, and for seven months there was a very real question as to whether there would continue to be an *economic* community, let alone a political one. The Community weathered the boycott and returned to its transition-period agenda, but it was on its guard against more trouble. A slight heart attack is poor conditioning for a severe one, although it can inspire a patient to caution.

The history of steps toward European union, however, need not suggest pessimism. After each checking of progress, there has been a consolidation of gains and a new advance. Nationalism still exists that can check the movement again, but nationalism has been overcome in Europe before. The fear of Soviet aggression that helped unify Europe after the Second World War has no counterpart in contemporary Europe, but there are compensations. Progress toward unity is more credible now than it was then, since so many successful beginnings have already been made. And, too, habit may maintain what fear helped create.

European leaders continue to demonstrate interest in political union. It is an apparent paradox that Europe can pursue the evolutionary approach to union, represented by the Common Market, and simultaneously debate a precipitate leap to union through the creation of a political community. The evolutionary approach may not be given a chance to show what it can accomplish not so much because of disdain for the principle as because of impatience for political unity. The élan of the Europhiles cannot guarantee the achievement of a political union, but it is good insurance that the economic objectives of the Common Market will be achieved.

Will Europe unite? That is a question whose answer is too portentous to be awaited quietly. Intellectuals on both sides of the Atlantic have advanced hypotheses about the dynamics of regional integration in an effort to discover the science of how a continent can be caused to grow together politically and to foretell the future of the Common Market and of its imitations abroad.[10] They, the Eurocrats, and other European citizens await the unfolding of Europe's extraordinary human experiment with equal excitement.

[10] A useful introduction to the literature and authorities in this field is *International Political Communities, An Anthology.* Garden City, N.Y.: Anchor Books, 1966.

Bibliographic Note

General

Literature on the European Community improves each year, and so bibliographies become obsolete rapidly. The periodical listing of new writing that is most focused on the Community is *University Research and Studies on European Integration* published by the European Community Institute for University Studies, Brussels, and the Community advertises all of its own publications through its annual *Publications of the European Communities,* Brussels. The Community publishes material in inverse proportion to its political importance, and such evidence of its internal politics as press releases or copies of draft proposals must be requested from the appropriate Community bureaus outside the normal information service of the Community. The printed materials of the Community that are most apt to relate to politics are the EEC monthly *Bulletin,* which includes policy proposals of the European Commission; the Community's *Journal officiel,* which includes regulations, parliamentary questions, rules of procedure, and court decisions; the *Annuaire* of the European Parliament, which catalogues its own structure and enactments and the enactments of the Council and the Commission; and the *Débats* and *Documents* of the Parliament, which constitute an extensive repertory of discussion on the whole range of constitutional and policy problems of the Community. The annual *General Report* of each of the three executives gives a concise survey of Community activities. An authoritative and concise *Handbook on the European Economic Community,* New York, 1965, was edited by Gordon Weil of the Community's Information Service, and a useful summary of the Common Market by a private person is U. W. Kitzinger, *The Politics and Economics of European Integration,* New York, 1963. The *Agence Europe,* Luxembourg, publishes the most informative private periodical devoted exclusively to the Community.

Chapter I

The history of the European unity movement is in Arnold Zurcher, *The Struggle to Unite Europe 1940-1958,* New York, 1958; the role of key powers in steps toward unity is in F. Roy Willis, *France, Germany, and the New Europe, 1945-1963,* Stanford, Calif., 1965; the interplay of selected social forces in the fifties is treated in Ernst Haas, *The Uniting of Europe: Political, Social and Economic Forces,* Stanford, Calif., 1958; European antecedents in economic cooperation are reviewed in W. O. Henderson, *The Genesis of the Common Market,* Chicago, 1962; and the negotiations leading up to the Rome Treaty are covered in Richard Mayne, *The Community of Europe,* New York, 1963. The experience of the Coal and Steel Community must be counted in the background of the Common Market, and its institutions are described in Hans Schmitt, *The Path to European Union,* Baton Rouge, La., 1962. Its activities are described in William Diebold, *The Schuman Plan: A Study in Economic Co-operation 1950-1959,* New York, 1959, and Louis Lister, *Europe's Coal and Steel Community: An Experiment in Economic Union,* New York, 1960. The Common Market's sister institution in the nuclear field is surveyed in Jarslav Polach, *EURATOM: Its Background, Issues and Economic Implications,* Dobbs Ferry, N.Y., 1964.

The most authoritative brief summary of the Rome Treaty is J. F. Deniau, *Le Marché Commun,* Paris, 1961, and a complete *explication du texte* is found in Alan Campbell and Dennis Thompson, *Common Market Law: Text and Commentaries,* London, 1962, its *Supplement,* London, 1963, and in the Commerce Clearing House, *Common Market Reports,* Chicago, 1962. Modifications of the institutions entailed in the fusion of the three communities are the subject of the "Traité instituant un conseil unique et une commission unique des communautés européennes et documents annexes," Brussels, 1965.

Chapter II

The Council is secretive in practice and eludes the interest of idealistic European scholars, who see it as foreign to the Community in spirit. The first book to appear on the Council was P.-H. J. M. Houben, *Les Counseils de ministres des communautés européennes,* Leyden, 1964, and light was shed on the nature of the Council by Leon Lindberg, *The Political Dynamics of European Economic Integration,* Stanford, Calif., 1963.

Chapters III and IV

The Commission is even more secretive than the Council, and the only printed information on its internal operations comes from the memoires of a retired commissioner, Robert Lemaignen, *L'Europe au berceau: souvenirs d'un technocrat*, Paris, 1964. Attitudes of active commissioners toward the Community are reflected in such writings as Walter Hallstein, *United Europe, Challenge and Opportunity*, Cambridge, Mass., 1962, and Pierre-Oliver Lapie (of the High Authority), *Les Trois Communautés: Charbon-Acier, Marché Commun, Euratom*, Paris, 1960.

Lemaignen and Lindberg both discuss the policy-planning process, which is the chief administrative responsibility of the Commission.

Chapters V and VI

More has been published on the European Parliament than on any of the other institutions. A thorough description of the structure and powers of the Parliament by a civil servant of the Community executive is Henry Manzanares, *Le Parliament européen*, Paris, 1964, and description of considerable insight by an employee of the Parliament is Pierre Genestet, *L'Assemblée Parlementaire européenne*, Paris, 1959.

Possible methods for direct election of the Parliament are the subject of Assemblée parlementaire européenne, *Vers l'election direct de l'Assemblée parlementaire européenne*, Luxembourg, 1960, and Wolfgang Birke, *European Elections by Direct Suffrage*, Leyden, 1961.

Commentary on the Parliament by its own Political Committee is in *Report on the Powers and Competence of the European Parliament*, Luxembourg, 1963, and the *Débats* and *Documents* published by the Parliament constitute the majority of the political documentation of the Community. Guy van Oudenhove has written on *The Political Parties in the European Parliament*, Leyden, 1965; and a monograph on a pressure group of the Community is Colin Beever, *European Unity and the Trade Union Movement*, Leyden, 1960.

Chapter VII

Institutional and political facets of the Court are covered in Werner Feld, *The Court of the European Communities: New Dimension in*

International Adjudication, The Hague, 1964. The court's *Recueils de la jurisprudence de la Cour* contain its case material.

Chapter VIII

The vast interest of outsiders in the Common Market expresses itself in numerous treatises on the relations between the Community and their own nations. Important among the writings on the issue of British membership are:

Concerning the merits: Colin Clark, *The Common Market and British Trade*, New York, 1962; A. Lamfalussy, *The United Kingdom and the Six*, London, 1960; Anthony Nutting, *Europe Will Not Wait*, London, 1960; John Pinder, *Britain and The Common Market*, London, 1961; and E. Strauss, *European Reckoning*, London, 1962.

Concerning the negotiations: Nora Beloff, *The General Says No*, Baltimore, Md., 1963; Miriam Camps, *Britain and the European Community 1955-1963*, Princeton, N.J., 1964; and European Economic Community, *Report to the European Parliament on the State of the Negotiations with the United Kingdom*, Brussels, 1963.

An assessment of Common Market relations with associates is Arnold Rivkin, *Africa and the European Common Market, A Perspective*, Denver, Colo., 1966; with would-be associates, W. B. Cunningham, ed., *Canada, The Commonwealth and the Common Market*, Montreal, 1962; and with peripheral nations not expected to associate, Pan American Union, Department of Economic Affairs, *The Effects of the European Economic Community on Latin America*, Washington, D.C., 1963.

Leaving aside the numerous books on Euro-American relations under the heading of NATO or Atlantic Union, in the abstract, several essays have appeared on the generalized topic of Euro-American relations: Max Beloff, *The United States and the Unity of Europe*, New York, 1963; Charles Cerami, *Alliance Born of Danger*, New York, 1963; Christian Herter, *Toward an Atlantic Community*, New York, 1963; and Robert Kleiman, *Atlantic Crisis*, New York, 1964.

Focusing specifically on Euro-American trade reform in the framework of GATT and OECD are James Allen, *The European Common Market and the GATT*, Washington, D.C., 1960; Emile Benoit, *Europe at Sixes and Sevens*, New York, 1961; Committee on Economic Development, *Trade Negotiations for a Better World Economy*, New York, 1964;

Randall Hinshaw, *The European Community and American Trade,* New York, 1964; Stanley Metzger, *Trade Agreements and the Kennedy Round,* Fairfax, Va., 1964; and Pierre Uri, *Partnership for Progress,* New York, 1963.

A European view of foreign relations is given by the book of lectures by Max Kohnstamm, *The European Community and Its Role in the World,* Columbia, Mo., 1964; but little can be expected from European authors, who are apt to regard external relations as external to themselves. Some selected foreign commentary on the Community is collected in Lawrence B. Krause, ed., *The Common Market, Progress and Controversy,* Englewood Cliffs, N.J., 1964.

Chapter IX

The spell the Common Market has cast on trade talk around the world is covered in Sidney Dell, *Trade Blocs and Common Markets,* New York, 1963; Rouhollah Ramazani, *The Middle East and the European Common Market,* Charlottesville, Va., 1964; and Victor Urquidi, *Free Trade and Economic Integration in Latin America,* Berkeley, Calif., 1962.

Index